Success with Local Marketing

By John Maggio of Hawk Marketing

ISBN: 9781074636753
Copyright © 2019 John Michael Maggio
All rights reserved.

Dedication

This book is dedicated to my father, Michael Maggio. He always knew I could fly high like a hawk. Also, my children. They paid dearly as I spent so much time away from them writing this book.

Ocean City 1980

Special Thanks

Cat Harvey, thank you for your time and grace as you helped us create this special project. Every Friday morning, month after month.

Lisa Cruz, thank you for being there when a friend needed help. When I was at my lowest, you had my back.

Rusty Rucks, thank you for helping me countless times in the past. Now, I can help so many in the future.

Thank you for the continued support and inspiration;

Susan Wheatley
Steve Hall
Michael Friedman
David Anderson
Chuck McDonald
Pat Voelkel
Robert Gazic
Paul Riecks
Jeff Whipple
Robert Bridges

Table of Content

PREFACE

Change can be heart stopping. Just the thought of change can cause stress and anxiety. This book is a story of how high we bounced after hitting rock bottom and all the great things we learned along the way.

Most of us have something standing in the way of breakthrough success. For me, it was serious anxiety. Not the kind of anxiety that tingles your nerves; but the heart-stopping kind that keeps you in your home for months at a time.

Today, more professionals are telling their stories about overcoming crippling fear and anxiety. These stories bring hope and encouragement to many. I'm going to share my story about how I decided to never let fear win again. It's important for you to hear this, as it serves as a backdrop for everything I've learned and gained from local marketing.

As a child, I was a mix of awkwardness and hyperactivity. As early as elementary school, I gained the nickname "Motormouth Maggio." Unfortunately, the name fit as I continually tried to blend in with the other kids. Our neighborhood, Cape St. Claire, was very large. With the high school being in the center, our community was much like a small town. In other words, everyone knew everyone else… and their business.

It seems I was good at attracting attention; it just wasn't always positive. My constant attempts to fit in often backfired. Looking back, I realize my hyperactive personality was polarizing. People either liked or disliked me, with no gray area in between. Because of this, I was often not as nice to my peers as I should have been. Sometimes I was being picked on, and sometimes I was picking on others.

Like many children with hyperactivity, poor grades excluded me from sports programs. However, I was a leader of the High School's engineering team.

At the peak of my high school career, something unexpected played out in eleventh grade. Out of what seemed like the clear blue, something pivotal happened. During morning announcements, a student announced the winners of the Homecoming Court. Two seniors, a

King and Queen, and eight juniors made up the court. Somehow, out of nowhere, my name was called! I was named one of four homecoming princes. I remember being very surprised and full of joy.

My moment came... the Pep Rally! The entire school entered the basketball gymnasium. The parents, teachers, and students filled the bleachers to the brim. The homecoming court was dressed in white shirts and ties. My mother met me on the bottom bleacher, to the left of the microphone. As the ceremony proceeded, my mother started to record the event on her camcorder.

The Vice Principal kicked off the rally. The crowd was fired up and cheered on and on. Then he started to announce the homecoming court. Prince number one... cheers, prince number two... cheers. Then he announced John Maggio. Immediately from the ranks of the football team came a barrage of boos. Within one second the entire auditorium joined in and booed.

The impact of that sound booming through the auditorium was like a death shot in my heart. Stunned, I remember putting my head down, fiddling with my tie and walking back to my seat... ceremony incomplete. They continued to announce the rest of the court with cheers. I turned to my mother. "Did you get that on the recorder?" "No," she said. "The camera didn't work right." When reminding my mother twenty-five years later about the event, she said it was a day and feeling of pain she will never forget.

After the pep rally on Friday came the homecoming parade and football game on Saturday morning. As members of the homecoming court and part of the parade, we were driven on a float to the football field in time for the game.

Right before the game, the court was announced one by one in front of the community, spectators, and parents. Once again, I was booed! This time, I walked off the football field.

Homecoming Game 1994

I was already headed down the wrong path, and it didn't take long for me to act out. Within weeks, for the first time, I was in trouble at school. I got into an altercation with another student on school property. His father, the Head Navy Football Coach, was none too thrilled. I was expelled immediately. Typically, a student would be allowed to repeat the grade the next year, or even attend another school in the county. That was the precedent at the time. Instead, I was told not to come back. As much as my parents tried to get me back in school, nothing could be done.

I lost my opportunity to compete in the engineering program sponsored by the leading firm in the state. We had just won the county competition and were headed to the state level. I had been deprived of the last chance of scoring a "touchdown" for my father while I was in High School.

It was just a matter of time until things went south for me. Small troubles with the law, bad breakups, and a close friend's death changed my state of mind. Looking back, I can tell you now I had a mental episode that lasted years. I was constantly obsessing about these failures and how people felt about me.

A pivotal point in my trouble with anxiety was an episode of food poisoning that I contracted at a local restaurant. Suddenly plagued with intestinal distress, I had to leave the table right away. After over a dozen visits to the restroom, we had to leave the restaurant. I even had to pull over on the way home.

After that moment, I felt trapped. I would not leave my safety zone. Every time I left my comfort zone, I felt sick and had to use the restroom... immediately. Over the years, there were several stretches of time that I could not even leave the neighborhood. Heading into town to accomplish simple tasks was often torturous.

By now, I constantly had panic attacks, and daily routines were extraordinarily difficult. Frequent rushes of adrenaline left me in a daily fight or flight mode. I was either paralyzed by fear or reacting to it by losing my temper. This became a daily occurrence.

Through my 20's and 30's, I was constantly misdiagnosed with bowel problems. The doctors put me through IBS, Crohn's, and Diverticulitis screenings, including colonoscopies. No worries, one of my best jokes is about the time I took my colonoscopy prep on the wrong day.

I remember the time my Uncle Keith gave the family a fishing trip as a Christmas gift. The trip was planned for April. Almost five months away! I remember having a panic attack every day about that trip until we left the dock. Like every other instance, once I was in the experience, all was fine. It was the lead up to the experience that always had me paralyzed.

Chesapeake Bay Rock Fishing April 2015

Just a few short months later, when I thought things couldn't get worse, my father was diagnosed with stage four lung cancer, and it had spread to his brain. The prescribed treatment was brain surgery. After the surgery, the swelling in his brain caused him to go off his hinges. My Uncle from Florida passed away and left my family his estate to sort out. On top of all this, the relationship with my boss at the time deteriorated quickly. Between my personal distractions and the tension with my boss, it wasn't long until I was terminated.

Finally! I had hit rock bottom! The very next day, I went to the emergency room and admitted myself. After a close evaluation, my doctor informed me that for years, I had been misdiagnosed. I did not have a gastrointestinal problem. I had a serotonin problem. My levels were shot!

He prescribed a small dose of Zoloft, and within days, I was free from my chains. My stomach pain was gone.

Having panic attacks for all of those years had left some pretty deep scars and some big messes to clean up. I started counseling and went every week for the following hundred weeks. I'm grateful for the journey, which has given me a unique perspective. Shortly after that, I attended my very first networking event. The rest is history.

There's no reason you can't go after your goals and dreams. You can have a successful business and a rewarding home life. Whatever you think is holding you back, it is just an illusion. I wrote this book for you. It's a collection of all the advice I've learned from the many people who have helped me on this journey. Apply it to your life and pass it on to others. Community is the answer to all of your marketing needs.

Chapter 1
A Marketing Mindset to Win

If you don't have a plan, all you have is a dream. Having a marketing mindset to win means keeping your mind positive, maintaining momentum, and staying on track.

Big Goals Lead to Big Success

If you want to have awesome success in achieving big goals, you must have a PLAN. A BIG PLAN! It has to be bigger than any plan you've had before.

If you've achieved the same goal before... that's not the type of goal we are talking about. If you accomplished a goal last year, and you want to do ten percent or fifteen percent better... that is not the type of goal we are talking about. You can plan for that, strategize and find a way from day one.

The type of goal we are speaking of is much bigger than that. It is a big goal, and you probably have NO IDEA how you are going to achieve it. This is the type of goal that will stretch you to your limits, and help you reach places you've never imagined. This goal is BIG and singular.

The main reason to have such a goal is that your belief in accomplishing the goal has to be so great that every decision you make for the next year, or the next few years, will revolve around that goal and get you one step closer.

Your financial advisor will tell you that those without plans never retire. Those that don't have one, three, five, and ten-year plans don't often succeed. Not to say it's impossible, but just much less likely. Many do not plan and save because they cannot feel, touch, or imagine themselves in that state of retirement. Emotional attachment to the word "retirement" is not there.

Here are ways for you to get deep into your goals and feel the emotion of accomplishment before it even happens.

Draw Your Dream

Local to Annapolis, Maryland, Lifelong Educator Liz Clickner taught me to draw my dream on paper. She told me to draw it in great detail. Draw your dream house, for example. The house, the cars, the boat, the gardens, the landscape.

Drawing and writing our dreams not only solidifies them, but it also releases chemicals in our bodies that help us feel positive and motivated towards those dreams. Once complete, place your drawing on your Vision Board and look at it every day. If you don't have a Vision Board, start one today! More on Vision Boards later.

Use Your Goal Card

Write your goal down on a card and laminate it. Carry the Goal Card around with you everywhere you go and place it in your front pocket. Read your Goal Card every morning, every night, and throughout the day.

Every time you go into a meeting or are about to face a challenge, reach down and touch the Goal Card in your pocket. This action will send a chemical signal to your brain that will boost your confidence and keep you on track. I was fortunate enough to learn about this trick early on from a gypsy, and later by a professional coach, Andrew Shaffer. This time-tested tool makes a real difference to your success.

Start A Mind Map

Earlier, I asked you to design a goal you have no idea how you are going to accomplish. Mind Mapping is a great technique to work through your ideas and brainstorm solutions.

Write your goal in a circle in the middle of a whiteboard or a piece of paper. Draw lines coming out from the circle - think, "spider legs." Some examples of ideas to write on the lines include the location, the date of your goal, the people needed to partner with, the names of network partners or contractors. Think of as many details as you can. But remember, the plan does not have to be perfect to move forward.

Vision Board

Designing a Vision Board helps you work towards a goal by giving you a visual representation of what you're working for. It's a great motivator because it reminds you every day what you're striving to accomplish. You've drawn your goal, you've written your goal.

Now, find pictures, quotes, drawings (yours, or ones that align with your goal). Get in touch with what your goal will look and feel like, and make it into a physical combination of your thoughts and feelings surrounding your goal. It should make you feel emotional. This chemical reaction will be instrumental in your success.

Affirmations

Affirmations are a great way to train our subconscious mind. Ninety-five percent of our actions are reactions which are based on our paradigms... our belief systems. For most of us, old beliefs get in our way and keep us from making progress. We struggle and fail to reach our goals because of our fears and self-imposed limitations. Using affirmations to tell your subconscious the way you want to be and perform is the best way to achieve success.

Unfortunately, this is one of those things in life that is so simple that it is often disregarded as too simple or silly. Don't buy into that way of thinking.

Start by writing down five or six affirmations on a piece of paper and read them twice a day. If you don't know what a good affirmation is or what to say Google "top 100 affirmations." Choose a few and take them for a test drive. Remember, you can always change or add affirmations as the year goes on. The important part is to develop the habit of reading them. Write them down as if they have already happened. Read them out loud for greater impact.

Morning Journaling

"The first ritual that you do during the day is the highest leveraged ritual, by far, because it has the effect of setting your mind, and setting the context, for the rest of your day." - Eben Pagan, Investor and Entrepreneur

Journaling in the morning sets aside time to think, plan, create, dream, and set the tone for the day. If you're looking to add some positive habits to your life plan, start with journaling, and kick off your day with some fresh thoughts on paper.

It doesn't matter what format you use. I use a guided journal called "Morning Sidekick." You can start a gratitude journal, work in a planner, or just fill blank pages. Try a couple of things, but start allowing time for this valuable effort first thing in the morning.

Don't Reinvent the Wheel

Ingenuity is a great thing, and it certainly has its place in marketing, but lean on the proven methods of those who have walked this path before you. This game has been played for a long time, and many people have worked hard to develop techniques and strategies that will help with your marketing mindset.

When I talk to you about getting coffee, this marketing method may seem old-fashioned or time-consuming. The thing is... it works!

Eat Your Frog

Write down the most important thing you need to accomplish today to move closer to your ultimate goal. Eat That Frog is a famous book by Brian Tracy. When he talks about "Eating that Frog," he is referring to developing a habit for management of your time and energy.

"The Frog" is that thing you need to do that is not especially fun, but very important. Chances are, you know what I'm talking about. Procrastination is a real problem for most people. But, FOCUS is the key to achieving success.

Attack this most important task that you are avoiding first thing in the morning, and free up your day from this pressing distraction.

You Are NOT Going to Fall Down

Get Ready for Tough Times. If you have a dream, a passion, or if you're on a journey, you will weather several harsh storms. But, it is very important for me to remind you not to get discouraged. You won't see it at the time, but this moment of disappointment will be a moment of growth.

Let me remind you of a time when you were younger- a time when you lost a job, maybe. You may have wondered how you were going to get by. Maybe you were scared that you wouldn't be able to pay bills, maybe you were even worried about how you would eat.

A few weeks later you had a better job making more money and had really grown. Did you fall and have to get back up? Did you fall or STEP UP?!

Looking back on your own experiences, you can see that many of those times enabled you actually to grow and gain precious ground.

One Door Closes, Two Open

I know you've probably heard some version of this before. It's absolutely true! It's hard to know whether something is working for or against you sometimes until you are further down the road.

Assuming that your next opportunity is right around the corner is a great strategy. The fact is, that assumption often drives the outcome. A positive mindset will bring positive results.

Henry Ford said, "Whether you think you can, or you think you can't, you're right."

Be ready to receive the opportunity when it shows up. Be grateful. Gratitude is the best way to maintain your positivity and encourage opportunity to knock on your door.

Have Some Perspective

Keep things in perspective when it comes to building your business. Don't panic when things don't go your way. Existing in a scarcity mindset, worrying about every marketing step you make to grow your business, will trip you up in the long run.

Adopt an abundance mindset, show gratitude for good things in your life, and focus on your goal and the corresponding plan.

Many of our parents or grandparents fought in major world wars. I am proud to tell you that both my Grandfather, Joseph Maggio, and his brother, Harry Maggio stormed the beaches of Normandy. Both were awarded purple hearts. Compared to them, what was I nervous about?

There are No Failures, Only Experiences

There is only one mistake you can make. Not trying. Sitting on the couch, scared. If you try, at the very least, you have an awesome learning experience. Keep making "mistakes." Taking shots is the only way to score.

How Do You Eat an Elephant?

The answer, of course, is "One Bite at a Time." Break your huge project into smaller tasks. It's okay to test and tune as you go. Adjusting the plan is always okay. Try not to adjust the goal.

You can't be afraid to jump in and take risks. Being in business has its ups and downs. It's part of the landscape, and you must be fearless, or pay the price for inaction or indecision.

Terror Barriers

Stop letting excuses keep you in your comfort zone. Every time you want to try something new or take a risk, this huge barrier appears and makes it seem impossible to continue. Written in huge letters, the barrier says; what if - I can't - I'm too scared - I'll fail. This barrier pushes us right back into the place we wanted so badly to get out of... our uncomfortable, comfort zone.

Let me tell you how thin your terror barrier is. Imagine a Little League homecoming football game. The football team is about to run out of the inflatable tunnel. The parents have a huge piece of paper spread across the opening. As the Fog Machine starts to cloud the air, the team suddenly bursts through at full speed. The paper tears with ease! The children are elated and already feel accomplished. What a burst of adrenaline right before the game! With that energy, there could have been a barrier every ten yards, and that team would keep running right through them all.

As large in appearance it may be, your terror barrier is paper thin. Remember, it's all in your mind. Next time the terror barrier comes up, reach out, take a swipe at it. Your hand will go right through.... Just like paper!

Don't be pushed back into your comfort zone. Learn to hate it there. You've been trying to leave it for years, so why do you keep rationalizing with yourself to stay? Why do you keep telling yourself a "ration of lies"? You can break through your terror barrier.

There Are No Perfect Plans... Take Action

Keep in mind that things don't always go according to plan. It's a good idea to have a Plan B. Sometimes, in mid-play, the quarterback has to run an audible. Don't plan too long or too far ahead because, in real life, ____ happens. Local Realtor, Donna Deter reminded us that, "Man Plans, God Laughs."

The most important thing is to take action every day. To take one step forward, no matter the size. Three hundred and sixty-five little steps forward will be one big celebration a year from now.

Every Prospect Pays You

A good friend, Pat Voelkel, used to sell cars at Honda of Annapolis. He reminded us of an old used car salesman saying, "Every Prospect Pays You," to stay positive in the face of rejection.

Routinely, customers would come on the lot looking for a car, ultimately saying "no." Pat was very patient, and knew that one out of twenty would buy a car. He knew that when he sold that car, he would earn $2,000.00. In a hurry to hear his yes, he was fine with those who said "no." He knew that with every rejection, he was that much closer to his goal.

To stay upbeat, Pat would take a $100 bill and place it in his pocket. Every time a customer would walk on the lot, he would tap his pocket or reach inside and touch the bill. He was giving himself a positive reminder that he was on the way to his goal. With a big smile, he would thank those who said no. A co-worker asked; "Pat, why do you seem happy even though they said no?" He would reply, "Because I am that much closer to my yes."

Never Chase

Don't waste time chasing people or trying to force them into your product or service. Allow us to give you some food for thought when it comes to chasing your prospect.

Michelle and I used to sell shoes at New Balance. We found out early on that when we pushed someone into a purchase they didn't feel fantastic about they would end up with "buyer's remorse." They would look at the shoes every day and have a bad feeling associated with the purchase, the brand, and even the salesperson.

Chasing prospects can be a huge waste of time. Remember, it has to be their choice, to do business with you. Let them choose you. As you know, some prospects enjoy your attention but never intend to purchase.

Keep it moving, be yourself, and you will stand out in the crowd.

You've Got to Have Momentum

Remember the homecoming game, and the banner we spoke of earlier? If we walked up to that banner, we might not be able to push through. It is going to take some force, even though it's only paper thin.

What would happen if you stopped going to the gym after working out for a year? You would lose significant strength and give up all the ground you had gained. Worse yet, you would see all of those who didn't take a break have great results, while you practically had to start over. You would need to establish a routine and keep up the momentum.

Now that we are battle ready…Let's circle back to the beginning and see how all this got started!

Chapter 2
It All Started with #1881

It's important to be aware that everything can change in an instant. For me and my sister Michelle, that's what happened when our good gigs at a large local marketing company disappeared. Like many other people, we were disappointed when we lost our jobs as the company self-imploded.

We went to Baltimore immediately to file our trade name, so that we could start our new company, Hawk Marketing. Choosing a name was easy. You see, our Dad owned a company for years called Hawk Retrofit. I worked there as a Sales Manager until I became too overwhelmed with anxiety. On my birthday 2015, we learned of the stage four cancer diagnosis for my Father, so Michelle and I were honored to name the new company "Hawk" after his old one.

Working for Hawk Retrofit in 1999 at 10 Light St. Baltimore, Maryland.

Now Hawk Marketing was in business, but what were we going to do to build it? Before the move, I had been working on cold calling charts, and walk-in scripts, but that wasn't me.

Honestly, I don't think anyone likes doing those activities. They consume so much time and effort... and cause so many moments of rejection. And, the thought of going out in public was made worse by my ever-present anxiety. Before, I had been an internal sales manager. Nothing out in the "wild."

We pulled out our list of contacts from our old client file and emailed all of our contacts to let them know of our new business. I was so grateful to get a reply from Karen Bailey. I had served with Karen on the Board of the Goshen Farm Preservation Society. She said she had some ideas for us.

Karen served as a facilitator of the networking group called The Entrepreneurs Exchange. She invited me to a meeting at Union Jacks in Annapolis as her guest. I didn't want to seem unappreciative, but I was pretty sure that I didn't want to do that, as my heart was beating fast, even at the thought of it.

Sitting there with my limited options, I knew I had to work beyond the anxiety and go to this meeting.

I wasn't there long when a man approached me. He was wearing a white button-down shirt, a navy sports coat, and slacks. He had a BIG presence in the room. When you think "larger than life," you're talking about a guy like Steve Hall.

As we talked, he seemed genuine. I'm not sure exactly what he said to me, because I was too busy thinking how much I admired his persona. The way he was able to talk to the group, he was a natural role model and made me yearn to be relaxed and effective like him. I admired him and became determined to become better at public speaking.

As the luncheon went on, I met a couple of gentlemen named Michael Friedman and David Anderson and had a conversation with them. Mike was a real gentleman with a lot of experience. He was also quick with a well-crafted joke. His delivery was perfect, as he pulled you in with his soft-spoken voice before nailing the punchline. David was a great photographer who was very nice and always helpful. I even attended his photography workshops!

They were both easy to talk with. As I explained to these two gentlemen, as coherently as possible, what I wanted to do, they recommended that I talk to Susan Wheatley. Susan, it seems, was a bit of a folk hero in our local networking world.

This was my very first networking event, and an opportunity was already manifesting itself. It felt like I was being led to my next step. I wasn't sure how I was going to get there. At times, I wasn't even sure where I was going. The guys encouraged me, telling me a little about what to expect at one of Susan's meetings.

"Go three times and then ask Susan to have coffee." "Susan knows everybody." It sounded like a secret handshake. The honest truth is, I didn't go. The universe pointed me in a specific direction, and I ignored it.

Several weeks went by, and the next networking event I attended was the Crofton Maryland Chamber's End of Summer Bash at the Crofton Country Club. It was a hot, humid day. Everyone was sweating and looking for some shade that afternoon. In late August, five o'clock p.m. can be unbearable in Maryland with temperatures over a hundred degrees and humidity at one hundred percent.

As I sought shelter from the heat, I found Dave Anderson again chatting with another gentleman. After a few moments, both of them started telling me again about Susan Wheatley and her networking group at 49 West St. in Annapolis. Both told me, John, "Go three times and then ask Susan to have coffee. Susan knows everybody!"

This time, I went for it! At my first meeting in this new group, I stood up and recited my well-rehearsed 30-second commercial and felt confident. In fact, I asked to go first, as I did many times back then. That way, I didn't have to feel my nerves build as it came closer to my turn. The reaction from the group made me feel welcomed. At the second meeting, I felt even more confident in my presentation.

After the second meeting, and before I even went for the third time, Susan called me. I thought to myself, "WOW, I must have really impressed her!" Remember, I was supposed to go three times and ask her. I was thrown off guard as she said that she wanted to learn more about my business. Immediately I went into "sales mode." Although nervous, I couldn't say no to the opportunity.

We met at a coffee house, and as I sat there anxious, she quizzed me about my business and was taking notes the whole time I was talking. She was asking me question after question. She seemed very interested in what I was saying. My inexperience caused me to ramble on about my products and services. I was in complete features and benefits mode. She must have been numbed by all of the jargon I was throwing around.

Then I paused, mid-sentence. I noticed that the book Susan was writing in was two-thirds open. She had my business card attached to the page, with a number next to it, Number 1881.

"Stop, wait a moment," I said. "What's with the number?" I asked. She said, "This is what I do." Then she gave me a real gift, as she revealed her coffee system to me.

Here it is in a nutshell:

- She would collect the card of every person who attended her networking group.
- Taping the card into her book, she would commit to asking each person to have a one-on-one meeting, typically over coffee.
- During the meeting, she would make it all about them. She would ask them questions and be a good listener.
- She went back into her previous books and tried to find referrals and connections for all that she met with.
- At the very end, for a few moments, she shared what she did.

Each page in her notebook had notes, cards, and... numbers. What's more, she had five more books just like that one in her big beach bag. She flipped through the books for a few minutes and gave me three cards. "Call these people," she said.

In the front of each book, there was the name and number of each person in the book for quick reference. Next to several of the names on each page was what looked like the @ symbol. About a quarter to a third of the names on each page had the symbol. I asked, "What does that @ symbol mean?" Susan replied; "That's not an @ symbol; it's a lowercase "e" for enrolled." Susan had been successfully signing up visitors to her networking group for Melaleuca for years! All by listening, providing value, and at the end, sharing what she does. For every ten cups of coffee, she was enrolling three people as customers or representatives.

I was hooked, and that is how Hawk Marketing got started in networking. It was a fresh, exciting way to bring in new business. We brought a couple of clients from the old company over. With Susan's blessing, we started our networking group and started putting our lives back together again.

Chapter 3
Creating Your Coffee Sales Funnel

If you are new to networking, hopefully, you already know that you cannot "hard sell" the other members of the networking group. If you have experience with networking, you can spot the newer guys and gals from a mile away. Many start networking, but eventually lose interest or feel that they do not get the results they should.

Here's an old networking question to ask yourself before an event. How many people came to the networking event to sell something today? Everyone, yes? How many people came to the networking event to buy something today? No one, right? So, how is this going to work?

People Buy from Those They Like and Trust

The best advice here is to listen, listen, and listen some more to your prospect. That is how you learn about them. Did you know that listening to someone actually increases their trust in you and raises their self-esteem?

W.A.I.T.

Keep this acronym in mind…. It stands for WHY AM I TALKING? You should spend twenty percent of your time asking questions, and eighty percent of your time listening to answers. Repeat some of their statements to let them know that you are understanding. Take a few notes to show your level of care. Remember, twenty percent asking questions, eighty percent listening to answers.

Aggressive selling, AKA "convincing," causes buyer's remorse, high return rates, and low repeat referral rates. Customers who talk themselves into buying the product are happy to have made the purchase, feel good about the decision, and often refer you new business. The difference in "helping a customer solve a problem" with one of your solutions versus you "selling them something" is all in your questioning techniques.

Playing Tennis

Steve Hall said; "You've never won a game of tennis with the ball on your side of the court."

Envision a tennis match in your head. You serve first. Meaning you ask the first question. They hit the ball back. Meaning, they answered your question. Now hit the ball back to them and create a volley. Back and forth. Back and forth. You ask questions they hit back answers.

Remember, **If you are talking, they are not buying**. If they are talking, they are convincing themselves to buy from you. If purchasing from you is their idea, the chances for buyers remorse are significantly less.

Do Your Homework

The best way to solve a problem is to gather as much information as possible. Before you call or meet with a prospect, learn a few details about them. This strategy will serve you well in creating a genuine conversation when you meet.

Social media makes it possible to learn about a person before you meet with them face-to-face. Google them, look at their Facebook page, their LinkedIn, etc. If they have a website, visit it and get to know their products and services. It shows respect for them.

Why perform pre-call planning? This is how you build your list of questions for the one-on-one meeting. Don't be fake, but be a little coy. You are going to be asking some questions to which you already know the answers.

For example, you may see on their Facebook profile that they have children or pets. If you have children, then the two of you have something in common. But please, do not start the conversation by telling them that you looked them up on Facebook and saw that they have two kids named Michael, age ten and Sarah, age eight! That sounds very aggressive. Instead, you may mention that you have children and a little about them. Then ask, do you have any children? You already know the answer, but you need to allow them to answer in their own way. This will build rapport and trust between the two of you.

You may see on their LinkedIn Profile that you both went to the same High School or University. You may want to mention what school you went to right before you started your career. Then allow them to tell you that they did the same. Sharing some of those stories from your college days goes very far.

These little commonalities go a long way towards building trust and creating a bond. Allowing someone to tell their own story is a huge part of building a relationship. The best strategy is to be a good host and to guide the conversation in a positive direction.

Look for Connection Points

I love to fish. Everyone in my circle of influence knows I like to fish. I post fishing pictures and make sure fishing is a big part of my personal brand. It's not your typical worm on a hook type of fishing. There is no sitting around relaxing and drinking beers with your buddies. People who are into fishing at this level are serious fishermen.

I mention all of this just to point out the following. If I meet someone that also fishes at this level, there is an immediate bond. Instantly there is a connection because both of us are passionate about the same subject.

Quickly the conversation turns almost exclusively to fishing. We may trade stories, fishing spots, techniques... the conversation could go on and on. We may even go on a fishing trip or two.

Let me ask you this question? After all that fishing, chatting, and having a good time, who are they going to buy from? Me or my competitor?

Commonalities are easier to find than you may think. You don't have to be an expert fisherman to be good at networking. You will find that many of us have children, pets, and hobbies. Some of us like to hike, run, or play a sport. Many of us are passionate about charities. It's likely that you have a few things in common with your prospect. And if you don't? Maybe they are not a good prospect.

Stick to the Mission

VERY IMPORTANT - Remember what the mission is. We are on a search and rescue mission. We need to search out the pain or problem our prospect is facing and offer them a lifeline. Typically, after small talk, the answers start to get more in depth. Personal stories and feelings are shared more often and with ease.

Now is the time to start getting your prospect to talk about some of the issues they are facing. Things you may be able to help with. Don't feel like you have to pry. If something is bothering someone, more often than not, they are willing to share if they feel you can be a resource.

Once pain points are revealed, ONLY present the ONE product or service that can help them. You can mess the whole process up by "spilling your candy in the lobby." Too often, salespeople cannot wait to present their PowerPoint presentation.

The days of PowerPoint presentations that review an entire company's menu of products and services are gone. Think about it this way. The only people still using PowerPoint presentations are non-skilled salespeople working a system. This is very much like robo-calling or cold calling prospects. It's way too much effort and is more likely to annoy people rather than engage them.

The Power of Three Choices

When my sister Michelle and I worked at New Balance Shoes, we trained our sales staff in a non-traditional way. We did not allow the customers to pick out their own shoes. Yes, you read that correctly. The customer was not allowed to pick out their own shoes.

We would first measure their foot. Then tell them if they needed a Stability, Neutral, or Motion Control Shoe. (I bet many of you are puzzled) Every athletic shoe on the market is one of these three types, and many consumers have no idea. They are often wearing the wrong type. On top of that, seven out of ten people are wearing the wrong size shoe.

We would find out which type was appropriate for them and only show them three options. We would allow them to try each style on. From there, they decided if it was a good fit. Never four! If they tried the fourth pair, they could no longer remember how the first pair felt. This caused overload, indecision, and often ended in losing the sale.

Even though we picked the shoes, offering a choice of three allowed it to be the customer's idea to purchase. Making it their idea increased purchasing morale and reduced buyer's remorse. We would never offer one shoe claiming it to be the best. That type of pushy arrogance would put many customers off. Not only that, but if the shoe was not in stock, how would we then sell them the "second best" option that day?

I once had a cell phone problem and had to go to the store for a replacement. While describing my problem, the salesperson exclaimed that I should just replace my phone with the latest Brand X phone because it was "way better anyway." Was he saying my previous purchase was flawed? Was he calling me ignorant? I mean, I had done a lot of research about my phone, and it had a fluke error. I was taken aback and a little upset, I asked to speak to the manager.

I'll end this section with this thought. When you go to the gas station, they offer three choices of fuel. Regular, Medium, and Premium. Have you ever left the gas station upset about the one you chose?

On a side note, who is buying all that Medium Grade fuel?

It Must Be Intimate

Before and after networking events, you will often see people having their one-on-one meetings. They sit stuffed in a coffee shop, sitting next to a bunch of people. This strategy will not work well.

The location of your one-on-one needs to be intimate. If there are a bunch of people around that can hear me, how can I tell you any secrets? How can I talk to you about private issues... health, family, or financial? I don't want anyone to overhear that information.

So, if you want to reveal pain and get to know each other, it needs to be in a quiet, semi-private setting. Find a decent restaurant with a slow lunch. Make sure it is quiet, and no one is sitting right next to you. Hunker down in that last booth in the back and really get to know each other.

We spoke about how every ten or fifteen one-on-ones will result in new business or a referral. But not if you are just going through the motions. Not if you are running prospects through the mill like cattle on an assembly line. You can't simply go through the motions. You must have your heart and soul into networking and forming relationships.

Workshop 3.1
Working Your Coffee Funnel

Here is a measurable plan of action that you can easily put into play. One of the best parts of this plan is that you can track the results. The absolute best part is that you are about to meet some fantastic, talented professionals who will enrich your life and business.

A physical representation of this funnel works best for some, but others may want to go digital. In our office, we have a shelf with five sticky notes labeled as follows; Need a One-on-One, Waiting for Response, Scheduled, Not Interested, Met With.

Place each card you obtain from networking in the very first spot labeled, "Need a One-on-One" By working each card from left to right, you will mine them like gold through your networking funnel. When you're finished, there will be two piles - A pile of possible prospects that did not qualify and a pile of Gold! These are your prospects, referral partners, and your circle of influence.

Need a One-on-One

Like Susan, commit yourself to following up, and try and schedule a one-on-one meeting with each person you exchanged cards with during networking events. This is the way to turn those cards into prospects, customers, and collaborators.

When you reach out, let the person know that you heard what they said at a networking meeting and you want to learn more about THEIR business. Get them in sales mode. Do not approach them by saying you want to sell them something. Add validity by mentioning the date and event where the two of you met. This will remind them and lend legitimacy to your request. Remember, we all receive way too many solicitations and SPAM, so you need to stand out.

Pro-Tip: You can create a template and send a similar message to each person.

Waiting for Response

You have crafted your invitation and sent it out. Now while you wait for the reply, follow these steps:

If you do not get a reply within five business days, it is VERY IMPORTANT that you send a second invitation. Let them know that you're committed to meeting them.

The first may have been missed, and the second invitation will serve as a reminder that you are serious about learning more about THEIR business.

If after two attempts and ten days, they haven't replied, place their card in the Not Interested stack.

Scheduled

Simply stated, you have created an appointment to meet. Keep the card here until AFTER the meeting. When setting one-on-one meetings, rescheduling often occurs. It may take more than one attempt before you get to meet. Do your pre-call planning before your meeting. Look them up and see if you have any common interests or topics they are passionate about.

Not Interested

This category cuts a few ways. "Not Interested" can mean they aren't interested, or that you're not interested. Some business cards may end up here before you even schedule a one-on-one.

If you feel that you do not want to work with a person or build a relationship, it's ok to place that person's business card here without spending a lot of time on it. Trust your intuition, but don't prejudge.

If the person never got back to you after you made several attempts for a one-on-one meeting, chances are they are not interested. Don't pursue them. What may look like a good lead could be a huge waste of time. Move on.

The pile can also include people you have met with, but do not meet your criteria, or are not qualified as a potential Networking Partner or Prospect.

Met With

You had a one-on-one, and hopefully learned more about THEIR business. Here are a few things to remember during the initial meeting.

THEY GO FIRST – Interview them. Ask them personal and professional questions. This is not the time for you to be talking about yourself or your business. Twenty percent of the time should be spent asking questions, and eighty percent of the time should be spent listening to them.

Try to get them to talk about things that are upsetting them, causing roadblocks, or hindering their growth. On the flip side, ask them about what excites them or if they've had any recent victories.

After they have introduced themselves in more detail, you do the same. Except, only mention the products and services that would help them solve their problems or reach their goals — no need to go through your entire laundry list now.

Try to make connections with your other Networking Partners. It's probable that not every person is a prospect, but referral partners can be a valuable part of your marketing plan.

Now you have created a stronger bond. You have been able to talk about all the things you wanted to in your thirty-second commercial but didn't have time to. Remember next time you stand up for your thirty-second commercial; you won't need to babble on because you intend to have a one-on-one meeting with each person in the room.

Make Sure to Connect

To follow up, connect with your new Networking Partner on Social Media. Many connect on LinkedIn, but more and more of us are becoming friends on Facebook.

Add your new Networking Partner to your email list. Not to spam them with sales jargon, but to keep them in the loop and to educate. Providing valuable content through email is a good way to familiarize your prospect with who you are, and to show your value.

Completing Your Funnel

If you follow these steps, a result will occur. You will find that for every one-on-one that you have, there will be a result.

A certain percentage will result in a direct sale, and a certain percentage will result in a referral. The key is to figure out how many one-on-ones you need to create a result. Is it ten, twenty, or fifty? Once you find this number, you will be able to see exactly how much networking you need to do to achieve a result.

How many one-on-one meetings does it take for you to generate a referral or sale?

Workshop 3.2
Your Coffee Funnel Template

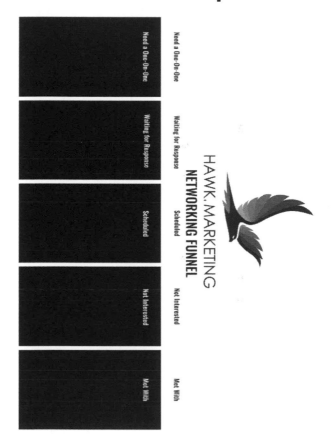

Chapter 4
Asking for a Warm Referral

I was feeling enthusiastic after a LinkedIn Workshop from Steve Hall, and another Aha moment occurred. Steve was showing us how to search our contact's connection lists to look for possible prospects. Maybe that LinkedIn contact would be willing to send out a warm introduction message to their connection. I asked myself, why not ask the people from networking for warm introductions?

Immediately I called Chuck MacDonald and asked him for a coffee. Everyone loved Chuck! With a bright smile and brighter disposition, you were lucky to have some of Chuck's positive vibes rub off on you.

Michelle and I met Chuck for coffee in Annapolis and proceeded to tell him what we had just learned and how we wanted to take LinkedIn out of the equation by simply using emails or text messages.

We told Chuck of a common problem that we were running into and how Information Technology Companies could be great referral partners for us. The reasoning behind this was they were often asked to create websites and deal with email addresses. We could make this assumption because Hawk was often asked to fix computers simply because our industries were often confused.

We asked Chuck how many IT companies he knew of from networking. He knew a handful. Then I suggested that I write a template so that all he had to do was copy and paste the introduction email and press send. He said, "no problem!"

Chuck sent out the introductions the next day, and within minutes, I had meetings booked.

Workshop 4.1

Warm Introduction Template

COLD CALLING SUCKS! The number of meetings you schedule, and the amount of effort you put out rarely adds up. If you are booking five meetings out of one hundred calls, you're doing fantastic! The average person is only successful three out of one hundred times.

Here is a practical way you can increase your averages to twenty-five percent and beyond. Instead of asking directly for a meeting with a stranger, ask for a referral from someone you already influence.

The simple math is as follows: If you ask twenty people to introduce you, ten will. Out of those ten, five people will accept your meeting.

A Few Notes Worth Mentioning

Continue to focus on motivation, pain, or pleasure. Your chances greatly increase if you have a reason to meet.

Make it easy for the person making the introduction. Write the introduction email for them so that they can edit or send it off without effort.

All too often, after an event, we receive emails from attendees that are sales driven. Please do not send a list of your products and services to everyone who attended. Those emails are erased immediately.

What Not to Send

(Only about 1% to 3% will open this type of message)

Dear Jane Smith,

I know you get these emails all day, but I think I have a shot? (sarcasm) My name is John Maggio of Hawk Marketing, and we recently met at a networking event. My company performs online marketing including; web design, email design, social media marketing, print design, digital media, consulting, search engine optimization, reputation management, call monitoring, and the list goes on and on... If you or anyone you know needs any of the services mentioned above, please reach out to me.

Insincerely, Jane Smith

Request for Introduction Template

(What You Send to the Referral Partner)

Dear John Doe,

Do you know any owners of IT companies from networking? I own Hawk Marketing, a digital marketing company, and I am receiving requests for their services lately. Often customers think digital marketing and IT companies can perform the same tasks. I am often asked to build a network, fix a computer, or install a phone system. As you know, there are several disciplines within the IT industry.

I am looking to build relationships with IT Companies so that I may refer this type of work to them. Do you mind sending Jane Smith an introduction email? To make it easy, I will provide the introduction email, and you can copy and paste it?

Thank You, John Doe

Introduction Template

(What the Referral Partner Sends on Your Behalf)

Dear John and Jane Smith

I wanted to take the opportunity to introduce the two of you. John Maggio is the owner of Hawk Marketing Services. John says that many customers often mistake their services with your services. Often asking him to build a network, fix computers or install a phone system. John mentioned that there are several disciplines within the IT industry, but often, the consumer sees all IT related companies as the same.

John was expressing interest in aligning Hawk Marketing with other Local IT companies, and that is when I thought of introducing the two of you.

I think it would be valuable for the two of you to grab a coffee and see if you can help each other out.

John, please reach out and see if you two can set up a time to have a quick meeting. If you would like me to be part of the meeting or if you have any questions, do not hesitate to call.

Follow Up

Respond right away! If you don't get a response, follow up in 5 business days with a hard, "Thank you for the introduction, John Doe. Jane, are you interested in meeting for coffee?" then let it be. Never chase. Also, use this technique each time you have a one-on-one. Always have a referral ask and a reason ready.

Workshop 4.2
Building Your Request Letter

Developing a Strategy

Before you start to design your letter, a little strategy is needed. Let's think about who your target audience is. What makes sense in terms of clients, collaborations, and strategic partnerships?

Let's say you own a marketing company as I do. I chose to target IT companies because people would assume that if I built websites, I must know how to do IT work. It's also safe to assume that IT companies would get inquiries from people that wanted to have websites built. Building a relationship like this represents a great referral partner and a great opportunity for strategic growth.

Someone who does the kind of work that a marketing company might need, such as writing, graphic arts, web development, photography, and videography... might consider reaching out to me to look for opportunities for collaboration.

List 5 Collaborations Within Your Network

1._____

2._____

3._____

4._____

5._____

Pro Tip: When you reach out, remember to be accessible and approachable. Offer a few dates, and one or two locations, preferably locations that are convenient to the other party. This will cut down on the back and forth necessary to set up the meeting. You want to make it as easy as possible for them to say yes.

Workshop 4.3
The Magic Referral Sheet

Use this worksheet to test and see if you can book 25 percent.

1. _____ referred me to _____ Meeting: Y N

2. _____ referred me to _____ Meeting: Y N

3. _____ referred me to _____ Meeting: Y N

4. _____ referred me to _____ Meeting: Y N

5. _____ referred me to _____ Meeting: Y N

6. _____ referred me to _____ Meeting: Y N

7. _____ referred me to _____ Meeting: Y N

8. _____ referred me to _____ Meeting: Y N

9. _____ referred me to _____ Meeting: Y N

10. _____ referred me to _____ Meeting: Y N

11. _____ referred me to _____ Meeting: Y N

12. _____ referred me to _____ Meeting: Y N

13. _____ referred me to _____ Meeting: Y N

14. _____ referred me to _____ Meeting: Y N

15. _____ referred me to _____ Meeting: Y N

16. _____ referred me to _____ Meeting: Y N

17. _____ referred me to _____ Meeting: Y N

18. _____ referred me to _____ Meeting: Y N

19. _____ referred me to _____ Meeting: Y N

20. _____ referred me to _____ Meeting: Y N

Total Meetings Booked: _____

Chapter 5
You Only Have Eight Seconds

Before we started training people to do an eight-second commercial, many folks had very long elevator pitches. These thirty-second commercials would often drone on into ninety seconds, and sometimes longer. At the time, everyone was talking about building the perfect thirty-second commercial.

Workshops were revolving around the subject, and professionals were even charging folks to help them craft their own. So, there I was, trying to build a system around my "perfect thirty-second commercial."

I remember writing and re-writing my speech, preparing to present it in front of a crowd. I would write what I thought was a good version, and then end up rewriting and fine-tuning my masterpiece... over and over.

No amount of editing helped. Every time I stood up to present my commercial, it felt very scripted, no matter how clever or engaging I thought it was. "Back to the drawing board," I would say to myself, wondering if I would ever be happy with the final result.

This journey would ultimately result in completely scrapping the thirty-second version and realizing that all you needed was eight seconds.

Gaining a Little Insight

One of my very first one-on-one meetings from the Entrepreneur's Exchange was with a gentleman named Paul Rieks. Paul had singled me out as a new business owner, as well as a rookie networker. We met at a local Panera Bread.

About this time, it occurred to me that I needed to find a mentor. Paul was older than me and seemed to be a great source of inspiration and advice. I wanted to be able to work with him on an ongoing basis.

Paul was a leader. He helped hundreds of entrepreneurs, young and old, throughout his career. His current venture, INSIGHT, was a peer-to-peer mentoring group that met monthly. A group of business owners would meet each month to discuss their victories, failures, and current issues to each other. Paul ran the group as the moderator.

Each month the members of the group would record what INSIGHT they had gained from the month's meeting and commit to an action they would accomplish by the next meeting.

With Michelle and I having to start our company suddenly, this group seemed like a good fit. The group consisted of approximately ten professionals, each unique in personality and profession.

One man, in particular, stood out. He was older, boisterous, and politely blunt. Jeff Whipple was a numbers guy and a career CFO. The two things he loved the most were cash flow strategies for contracting firms and old-time radio.

One morning, Jeff Whipple outlined the Nine Whys in a presentation he was giving the group.

They are:

1. To contribute to a greater cause, make a difference, or add value
2. To build trust or create relationships based on trust
3. To make sense out of things, especially if complex or complicated
4. To find a better way
5. To do things right or the right way
6. To think differently and challenge the status quo
7. To master things or seek knowledge
8. To create clarity and understanding
9. To simplify

These are the basic reasons "why" people do what they do. This information was eye-opening and made me think. As I looked at the sheet over and over again, I saw similarities within the reasons why. You could almost group them into personality types.

Sandler and the D.I.S.C. Assessment

We belonged to INSIGHT for several months before we started with Sandler Training. In the meantime, my relationship with Steve Hall and his budding sales manager David Wendkos was building.

Steve suggested that I take a DISC assessment. "An assessment?" I remember thinking to myself. Steve insisted that I would gain a vast amount of insight from the process. Trusting what Steve said, I agreed to allow David to administer the assessment for me.

The questions seemed strange to me. They revolved around how I felt about myself, how I wanted others to feel about me, and how I thought others felt about me now. The purpose was to discover my character traits. Once complete, we reviewed the results together.

That is where my first "Aha Moment" happened. I learned that DISC stood for Dominance, Influence, Steadiness, and Compliance (many versions exist, but this is what Sandler uses). Again, I noticed the groupings. In fact, this time, quadrants. Similar to my thoughts on the Nine Whys.

Each personality type has specific strengths and weaknesses. Each type was very much needed, with none better than another. A major insight in this training was learning what would upset or create pain for each of the personality types.

- Dominance would hate to lose.
- Influence would hate to be seen in a bad light.
- Steadiness would hate to be out of control.
- Compliance would hate to be wrong.

Michelle and I had opposing DISC assessment results. I was a DI, and she was an SC. I was amazed at the revelations from this test. Michelle and I took Steve Hall's advice and joined the Foundations Program at Sandler Training. Sandler specializes in relationship building and sales training. I figured this was a good place for us to train for our business. There was a lot of printed material, as well as a lesson about creating the perfect thirty-second commercial.

Painful Personality Paradigms

I learned that each personality type has distinctive fears. A given type of personality may make you predisposed to the fear of losing control. Or, maybe you are frightened of looking bad in public. Or any other fears that may be associated with particular personalities.

I began to overlay the Nine Whys over the four quadrants of the DISC assessment. It was then that I knew if I could hit three out of four quadrants during my elevator pitch, I could appeal to the majority of the room.

My second "Aha Moment" came when I realized that these are the real pains that people have their paradigms wrapped around. As I was trying to perfect my thirty-second commercial at Sandler, it kept getting shorter and shorter. I ended up cutting the BS out, and thinking, "It all boils down to the Platinum Rule."

The Platinum Rule

If you don't know, the Platinum Rule is the not-so-distant cousin of the Golden Rule. The Platinum Rule says that you should "Treat others the way that **they** would like to be treated." Simple and straight to the point.

Using an eight-second commercial instead of a thirty-second one may have come about as a result of my anxiety not wanting to drag things out, but the truth is... it works.

Less Is More

Use your eight seconds to go directly to the pain points your prospect is feeling, and offer relief. Keep it positive, keep their attention, and keep it moving. The goal is not to sell someone in those eight seconds. You're trying to get a coffee date, not a commitment.

Chapter 6
Your Eight Second Commercial

Some groups give you thirty seconds; some groups give you sixty seconds. You can take five minutes if you'd like, but NOBODY is listening after eight seconds. You have eight seconds to grab their attention and make an impact. Otherwise, attention is lost, eyes start to wonder, and people start looking at their cell phones.

Good news! Most of the networking magic happens after the event during your one-on-one meetings. That's right! The actual networking happens after the event. So, SAVE YOUR BREATH for the coffee meetings you are about to have. Not just for fun, but for funds. It's a numbers game. For every ten to fifteen one-on-one meetings, like a sales funnel, there will be a result: a new business, new leads, or a new referral.

If you've had coffee with someone in your networking group once, meet for another cup! When is the last time a good relationship ended on the first date?

Remember not to "show up and throw up." Save your breath! Skip the long boring elevator pitch, and switch to the eight-second commercial. Less is more. Use impactful words that send a cleaner, clearer message.

Don't spill your candy in the lobby... which is to say; don't stand up and spout out every morsel of service you offer. Don't reveal every feature and benefit of your product or service. You are way too premature. Slow down! This is about an introduction in hopes of getting a coffee meeting, not a sales opportunity.

Do your best to stay out of sales mode. Do not try to convince or force your coffee date to be a prospect. This behavior will create a Fight or Flight response (Usually a flight). It may not be obvious. A flight response may look like a polite request for more information, or a statement such as, "looks great, just not now."

The end result when you try to woo prospects that are just not interested... wasted time. You waste your time, and the "prospect's" time. This is the time you could spend talking to someone genuinely interested in what you offer.

Focus on Pain

People only spend money when one of four things happen.

- Pleasure right now
- Pleasure in the future
- Pain in the future
- Pain right now

I'm here to tell you, ladies and gentlemen, that often, prospects have their wallets out fanning the flames of pain right now. That is to say, they will be willing to pay for pain relief in these situations.

Be Effective

Allow us to lay this out clearly. A good eight-second commercial does four things effectively:

1. Clearly introduces you to the audience
2. Asks a question that gets the interest of the audience
3. Presents a strong call to action

4. Clearly introduces you to the audience again

The Parts of Your Commercial

Part 1 - The Introduction

Use a classic restaurant training technique. State your name at the beginning and the end of each interaction. People often can recall things said at those moments. In the food industry, if you want people to ask for you to be their server, you need to make sure they remember your name.

It's the same for any business. People want to know who they're doing business with. It's a proven fact that folks want to do business with people they like and trust.

Introduce yourself and your business. Loud and Clear. For example, "My name is John Maggio of Hawk Marketing."

Part 2 - Pain Question

Invoke an emotion. Introduce a pain, problem, or roadblock YOU KNOW is happening to your prospects. You need to ask a painful question or make a painful statement that will garner the most attention in the room. Again, this is a question you already know the answer to, and your audience does too. That is why this strategy is effective... it urges them to take action.

A financial advisor may ask; "Do you have enough money for retirement?" Since most people in our country have less than $5,000 in savings, the advisor already knows that most people in the room are not ready.

A health insurance salesman may ask; "Are you paying too much for healthcare?" Knowing the rates have skyrocketed, most people in the room will reply, "yes."

A life insurance saleswoman may ask, "Wouldn't it be embarrassing for your family to have to start a Go Fund Me campaign because you were unprepared at the time of your passing?"

Part 3 - A Strong Call to Action

After you have evoked emotion, give a call to action to show how you can help solve that problem. "If you are paying too much, let me show you how you can save!" "If you are not ready for retirement, let's work together and help you get back on track."

Some hints from the DISC assessment tool:

- For a Dominant personality; if you want to win one last time...
- For an Influential personality; if you want to look good...
- For a Steady personality; If you want to remain in control...
- For a Compliant personality; if you want to be right when it is most important...

Part 4 - Re-Introducing Yourself Again

Always start and end with your name. You'd be surprised how easily people will forget your name and company if you don't reinforce it during the conversation. Most people will tell you, "I'm not good with names."

End with... "Again, my name is John Maggio of Hawk Marketing!"

Building Your Eight Second Commercial

Let's help you develop your key question. Ask yourself a few things about your industry;

- What problems do my prospects have that I can solve?

- What goals do my prospects have that I can help them achieve?
- What roadblocks or detours do my prospects face, and how can I help them avoid them?
- What are common industry complaints?
- What are some of your industry stereotypes, and how are you different?

Identify your prospect's pain and focus on removing it effectively. Once your prospect sees you as a source of relief, they will now look to you for future solutions.

Think about the problem that your prospect has and how you can solve it. Get deep with it. With your expertise, you can explain their problems better than they can. When this happens, your prospect will trust you to provide the solution.

Get in touch with your unique selling proposition. Determine how you differentiate your product or service, and what makes you stand out. Maybe your personal brand or hobbies are the differentiator. It might be price, quality, conscientious service... Whatever it is, get in touch with that one thing, and build on it.

Think Blue Ocean, not Red Ocean. This refers to new markets and crowded, saturated markets. When you envision a Red Ocean think of a feeding frenzy. Several sharks after the same fish. If you are in a crowded market with lots of competition, think outside the box and create your own Blue Ocean. Do not do what everyone else is doing, or you will be lost in the sauce, offering more of the same.

If you don't want to be treated like a salesperson, then do not act like one. Reframe your thinking. Instead of selling a prospect this product or that service, you are going to help your clients solve their problems. You are helping and enabling people to improve their lives, solve problems, or achieve goals. But remember, it must be their idea.

Workshop 6.1
Building Your Eight Second Commercial

Find the Pain Points

Brainstorm and list all the problems that your prospects encounter. What are common complaints, stereotypes, and misinformation that often come up? Try to speak to issues that you know are happening to your audience.

1.

2.

3.

4.

5.

Workshop 6.2
Building Your Eight Second Commercial

Part 1 - Your Introduction Statement

Introduce yourself and your business. Loud and Clear.
My name is_____
of _____

Part 2 - Your Pain Question

As an example: "Are you experiencing pain, a roadblock and lack of results?"

_____
_____

Part 3 - Your Qualifying Statement and Call to Action

Example: "If you are experiencing this pain or need to overcome this roadblock, schedule a one on one with me after the meeting."

_____
_____
_____

Part 4 - Repeat Your Name and Company

Again, my name is _____

Of _____

Examples

1. When your toilet overflows out into the hallway, you'll be calling on the Father, Son, and the Holy Spirit. But, after ABEND repairs your toilet, you won't be saying AMEN, you'll be ending all your plumbing prayers with ABEND! Can I hear an ABEND? ~ Ron Kaylor of ABEND Plumbing

2. If your portfolio is a little down, perk up your investments with a little Coffey. ~ Stephen Coffey of Edward Jones

3. Home buying is a cinch with Doris Lynch. ~ Doris Lynch Williams, Realtor

4. If your loved ones need special care. Don't despair. Call A Man Who Cares. ~ Pat Voelkel, Senior Care Provider

5. If you have a cleaning problem, we have a cleaning solution. ~ Robert Wade of Maid Healthy

6. Friends don't let friends pay excessive bank fees! ~ Robert Gazic of SECU

   or

   Did you know that you do not have to be a State Employee to be a member of a credit union? ~ Robert Gazic of SECU

7. Most people pay too much for healthcare. We pool healthy people together, so they pay significantly less. I care more than Obama Care, your friend with benefits ~ Jim Procaccini of US Health Advisors

8. Do you know anyone that would like to try online marketing but does not want to sign a contract? Hawk offers marketing services with zero contracts, and you can cancel anytime ~ John Maggio, Hawk Marketing

Chapter 7
Your Networking Routine

Attitude is Everything

- Positive Thoughts Create Positive Feelings.
- Positive Feelings Create Positive Actions.
- Positive Actions Create Positive Results.

Are you facing a huge challenge? A milestone you are unsure of? How do you eat an elephant? One bite at a time! To keep a positive mindset, track your daily behaviors. Meaning, track your at-bats, not your home runs. Million-dollar professional baseball players miss the ball 70 percent of the time. Glass half full or glass half empty? It's up to you.

The most important thing is that you create a realistic schedule and stick to it.

Accomplishing activities such as attending networking events and having one-on-ones gives you a sense of accomplishment. You'll get a winning mindset, which creates positive momentum.

Judge yourself on whether you accomplish the daily activities. Be practical. Not every effort will yield success. Remember, what Pat Voelkel reminded us of, "Every prospect pays you!"

Keep it simple, and take the easy wins. Planning is great, but don't be caught in the trap! The trap of continuously planning and over planning and never taking action! "Paralysis by analysis" will set in.

Your Routine

You can only control your behavior. You may not be able to control the direction of individual sales or opportunities, but you can harness the power of averages to find success. To do this, you need to measure your actions and activities. If you can find a realistic daily regimen to engage in, you can not only be successful but feel successful the entire time.

Here are a few things to think about when planning your schedule.

Would it be easier to plan for one day or one month? Clearly it is easier to take it one day at a time. Would it be easier to accomplish the three most important items for the day or the twenty things on your to-do list?

Many professionals plan in one-week increments and limit their focus to one, two, or three tasks for their entire day! That's all? Yes, and if they accomplish those tasks, they certainly will keep working, but the point is, they didn't overload themselves with a huge list of tasks that are nearly impossible to accomplish. Also, they don't spend all their day concocting complex plans.

Remove emotion from sales success or failure. Do not be emotionally attached to the outcome. Remember, the prospect is the one that chooses you. Not the other way around.

If you are doing your planned activities for the day, you are winning. If you go to all the scheduled events you had planned for that week, you are winning. If you attach yourself too closely to sales numbers, you can find yourself feeling down. Your prospects and networking partners will see your grief. Don't let yourself slip into this cycle.

One of the best ways to avoid fatigue and generate success is to look for quality over quantity. Most of your efforts should be about qualifying your prospects. Chasing unqualified, low-quality prospects can leave you feeling frustrated. Endless follow-ups, shallow promises, and tons of time wasted.

When qualifying your prospect, try to identify the core challenges they face. If a prospect is not facing the challenges you have identified as your core services, move on (ask for a referral of course). Unqualified prospects are a huge waste of time, money, and effort.

That is why it is worth mentioning again. Do not chase, convince, or force. The prospect chooses. Present, follow up once, and move on.

Start from the End

To get started, try reverse engineering your goal to find your daily regimen. What's your goal? Maybe you want to bring home $100,000 in gross income? In general, pick an easy number divisible by ten. How many sales do you need to make this number a reality? How many presentations do you have to make those sales happen? How many phone calls or networking events must you go to book those meetings?

Take a moment to fill out the following;

1. What is your Income or Revenue Goal for the Year? _____

2. How many new clients do you need to achieve this number? _____

Finding your average. It is your total monthly sales divided by the number of new clients. **It does not "depend"!** There is always an average. If there is not enough data for a month, use a quarter year or a years' worth of data. For example; total annual sales divided by total number of clients/contracts.

3. To achieve the number of new clients you need, how many presentation meetings do you need to have? In other words, how many times must you present to a qualified lead to convert a new client? _____

4. To achieve your presentation goal, how many initial one-on-one coffee meetings, introductions or conversations must you have? _____

5. Divide that number by 52 weeks. How many conversations must you start each week?

    _____

6. Is this number realistic?   Y   N

Common prospecting activities include; telephone cold calling, cold walk-in, referral meetings, networking events, and follow up calls. Remember, you must conduct these activities with genuine intent. In other words, work with a bias towards results. You cannot leave ten voicemails with zero follow up and expect results. On the other hand, you cannot simply attend networking events and not engage.

7. So, how many of each of these activities do you need to perform to start the needed amount of conversations?

Cold Calls: _____ = _____ meetings?

Cold Walk-ins: _____ = _____ meetings?

Referral Requests: _____ = _____meetings?

Networking Events: _____ = _____ meetings?

Follow Up Calls_____ = _____ meetings?

Which activities are your most productive?

More Money... More Problems

When creating our company, Hawk Marketing, we performed a similar exercise. We looked at what it would take to achieve a million annual sales. How many clients it would take? How much would have to be delivered? How many people would have to be hired to create and implement assets? It started to look overwhelming and expensive, almost immediately. At the end of the exercise, the amount of physical work and mental stress it would take to achieve this amount was huge.

We discovered that there would be quite a few moving parts to reach that goal. First, we struck out to see how many sales we would need to complete to achieve this revenue goal.

We first found what our average monthly revenue would need to be. $1,000,000.00 divided by twelve months is $83,333.33 each month.

Then we sought to find how many clients we would need on retainer to achieve that monthly revenue. If our average client paid $1,000.00/mo, we would need eighty-four clients.

Now that we found how many clients we would need, we sought to find out how many actions it would take to convert eighty-four prospects. How many cold calls? How many meetings? How much networking? Before we got too far down that road, something else dawned on me. What would it take to handle eighty-four clients? A full staff, more equipment, a larger office. With all that overhead, how much were we going to profit when the dust settled? Having more moving parts means more risk.

Performing this exercise called for immediate change to our business plan.

#1 Our prices needed to go up if we ever wanted to achieve our goal. Like many agencies, we were underpriced.

#2 We realized we needed a different strategy to reach our revenue goal. We would need to deploy a product with a much higher price point and much higher margins. This is one of the very reasons we wrote this book.

Profits vs. Revenue

My father, who owned a window and door company called Hawk Retrofit would often come home and say; "I did a $5,000 job today!" It sounded great rolling off his tongue. My mother would always be right there to correct him. "Oh yeah," she said, "How much was the glass?" "What about payroll?" "Don't forget Gas and Insurance!" It should be no shock that many business owners and sales professionals do not take expenses into account when figuring their profits.

The reason I believe this occurs all too often is that most of us are good at what we do, but accounting isn't our strong suit. For most of us still in business, we have had to learn it the hard way, or we've employed the help of professionals... often both.

At New Balance Shoes, Michelle and I worked in a franchise store in the Annapolis, Maryland Mall. The owner and my mentor, Bob Bridges, had a degree with a minor in statistics. A child of the depression era, he would drill into our heads the costs of doing business.

As an illustration, let me give you some insight into the costs of doing business in that retail environment.

The average shoe cost to us was $50 a pair wholesale from New Balance. We would mark the shoes up and try very hard to sell them for $100 a pair retail.

Immediately, many of you automatically assume that we made $50. The actual profit was $10-$15. That was if you were a good operator. After paying for rent, payroll, marketing, electric, insurance, etc... In the end, the profit margin was a little above ten percent.

Some customers would often complain that we did not have many sales. Bob would tell us; "if we put them on sale for any more than ten percent off, I might as well stand at the front door and hand out money." Meaning, he would be losing money and would not only be a waste of time but detrimental to the survival of his business. Bob would rather not sell a shoe at all than to sell a pair on sale. Where most salespeople are concerned with selling as much product as possible in a month, Bob was ONLY concerned about profit. This leadership and mentality allowed him to make it through the 2008 recession. The store remained profitable until his retirement.

Chapter 8
Leveraging Mobile Apps

In the early '90s, many resisted computers. Folks thought they didn't need to adapt. Today, everyone walks around with one in their back pocket. Cell phone technology and the race to the "next best" has advanced our toolsets (and mindsets) greatly. Here are eight types of apps available both on Google Android phones and iPhones that can help us tremendously throughout our day.

#1 To-Do Lists & Note Taking

Taking notes, making lists, and adding contacts on the fly is crucial. Making sure you have the ability to record information with the swipe of your finger will come in handy daily. Here are a few popular productivity apps that sync seamlessly across your phone, tablet, or computer.

- Evernote - A great note taking app. Easy access and the ability to create to-do lists. Syncs across all your devices and operating systems.

- Trello - Organizes workflow and can be used for project management. Switch from list view to calendar view. You can use to do lists as well.

- Google Keep Notes and Google Tasks - Conveniently connects to your Gmail and can be viewed from your inbox. Syncs with your Google account so you can log in anywhere.

#2 Scanning and Faxing

Scanning documents into PDF files is as easy as taking a photo. This is very useful in the paperless era. Faxing... what? Yes, you read that correctly, faxing. Remember the first fax machines with thermal rolls of paper? Remember the sound of a fax machine? It's true, you may not need to fax often, but in some legal situations, the law requires things to be faxed.

- Tiny Scanner and Tiny Fax - These great apps allow you to move documents to the cloud, email them to yourself and others. And, you can even send the documents to a fax machine. Take a picture with your phone, and the app converts the photo into a PDF. Simple and DONE.

#3 Automation For Your Apps and Devices

Automation is a time saving, crucial part of your strategy. You will be surprised as to how many automation ideas "IF This Then That" has come up with using the software and hardware accounts we already have.

- IFTTT - A great app that helps to sync information across all devices and platforms. Post something in one app, and it automatically posts it in other apps. It has thousands of other automations. It's definitely worth exploring.

#4 Maps and Directions

Gone are the days of Map Books. Remember looking up the street in the back to find which page in the book your destination was on? Heck, some of you didn't know where you were going then, and still might not know now. One thing smartphones have nailed down is GPS Navigation and Mapping Apps.

- Waze or Google Maps - Get GPS, maps, directions, and traffic estimations in real time. Both are wonderful apps, and Google owns both. Waze, however, is the Pepsi to Google Map's Coke. Although Google bought Waze, they kept the two apps distinctly different. One of the major additions to Waze is the social media function. Users report incidents, accidents, and even police activity in real time. The tradeoff is that Waze uses more bandwidth and battery.

#5 Leave a Review

Leaving a review for a peer is a powerful networking gesture. Reviews help them stand out. If your peer or prospects are trying to stand out online, reviews help Google determine who is a good result. There's a pretty good chance they may leave you a review back or at the very least be grateful.

- Contribute by Google - Once it's own App, Contribute is now a feature of Google Maps. Contribute tracks your destinations and lists places that you have been. This makes it easy to leave several reviews in one sitting. Maybe leaving reviews might be part of your monthly sales ritual. The more reviews you give, the more points you earn. The longer the review, the more points. Add a photo and get bonus points. Just an added layer of entertainment to an area of networking in need of improvement. We are not leaving enough reviews for each other.

#6 The Mysterious Cloud

The secret to the Cloud is that there is no mystery. The term "cloud" ultimately confuses millions of consumers each day. Think of the cloud as offsite storage that you can access from your phone, tablet, or computer. Many are using this type of storage exclusively so they can access all of their files seamlessly at any location from any device. The biggest players in offsite storage right now are;

- Google Drive - Popular with Android and Gmail users.

- Dropbox - One of the first mainstream cloud brands. Most popular with Microsoft Windows, and Mac users.

- iCloud - Popular with Mac, iPad, and iPhone users.

- OneDrive - Introduced later by Microsoft, OneDrive comes preinstalled on all windows computers.

#7 Mileage and Expense Trackers

Don't let this data get away from you. Tracking your mileage and expenses throughout the year becomes crucial at tax time. Another important reason to track your expenses is to find out how much your cost of doing business is. Every drop of gas and every bite of food all goes against how much it takes to earn a profit.

- Mile IQ, Hurdlr, or TripLog - Track your mileage and transportation expenses with consistency. With free and paid versions, these apps will help you seamlessly track your information and allow you to export reports. Some are as easy as swiping left or right.

#8 Business Card Scanning Apps

Personally, I'd rather hand type each card in, because I can type rather fast. Otherwise, using a card scanning app can be a time-saving tool. Take a photo of the card, and the app will pull out all of the contact information for you to verify. Sometimes you'll have to make an edit, but overall the apps are very accurate.

- CamCard, Adobe Scan or Evernote Pro - Scan the business cards you collect and convert them into usable data. Build your email list or export contacts to your CRM. In some instances, these apps even send connection requests on social media. Some even allow you to take a photo of multiple cards at once.

And Many More...

Technology moves fast! In years to come, there will be faster, better, and more advanced technology. We wanted to give you an overview of how apps could help save time and increase productivity.

Chapter 9
Email and Automation

Email Marketing is Still #1

Give your customers what they want. When polled, over ninety percent of people wanted to receive an email from brands they have an interest in. Eighty-six percent wanted an email monthly. Shockingly, fifteen percent asked for daily emails.

Over 3.7 billion people are using email, and that number is growing fast. By 2021 the projected number of email users will exceed four billion. In contrast, in 2019, Facebook reached a little over two billion users. Email is crushing it!

Eighty percent of Retailers and B2C businesses report that email marketing yields the highest return on investment. On average, for every dollar spent, their return was between thirty-eight to forty-four percent.

All the cool kids are using email. With more and more of our future generations looking down at their phones, email usage is growing. Seventy-three percent of millennials prefer email when interacting with companies. Gone are the days of talking on the phone with big brands. Younger generations prefer digital interactions.

Automation, automation, automation. Work while you sleep! Over fifty percent of corporations are using some form of email for automated drip campaigns.

Parts of an Email

Subject Line - This must be catchy. Your subject line usually determines whether people will open the email. More companies are using emojis in their subject lines. Over half of users reported that using emojis to create catchy subject lines increased their open rates.

Here's a buzzkill. Using the word "donate" causes a fifty percent drop in open rates. A short, catchy subject line is crucial, and you must stand out in a crowded inbox if you want attention.

The Body - The point of sending an email is to attract people to your landing pages, blogs, or articles on your website. Getting the user away from their inbox and into your sales funnel is a priority.

What Should You Send?

How Long? - We only want to send a partial article. Encourage the user to click through to your landing page to view the entire offer.

Content - Get out of sales mode. Do not send ads, sales, or discounts. Do not send an overview of all the services that you offer. Try to educate your audience. The point is to remind them of you, not to offer them your services.

Call to Action - Use action words such as now, important, hurry, or urgent. Make your words or button stand out with size and color.

Pro Tip: Transactional Emails: Many of us get transactional emails. Such as order confirmations, receipts, invoices, etc. Transactional Emails are opened eight times more than solicitations. Think of these as a second opportunity to send a message. You could ask for a referral, introduce new information, offer a discount on the next purchase, suggest an add-on, or ask for a review.

Pro Tip: Use the option to include the person's first name in the email. Personalized emails get a five percent higher open rate.

What to Expect

- Fifteen - Twenty Percent Open Rates
- One - Three Percent Click Thru Rate

Automation

Most platforms, including MailChimp, offer Automation and Remarketing. An automated email or series of emails can be triggered by adding someone to a list, triggered by a date, or a series of dates.

For networking, many of you may want to use an automated email to send out requests for one-on-one meetings. Another automation idea is to send out a request for a Google review.

Many companies design a series of emails to distribute over time. Imagine a Yoga Studio drafting ten emails designed to show a new pose each week. Once subscribed, the recipient will systematically receive all ten emails one at a time, week after week.

The instructor did have to put more effort in up front but only had to do it one time. Now when they enter a new customer, they no longer have to worry about sending them the email series.

Chapter 10
Your Online Sales Funnel

Think of Your Website as a Sales Funnel. You load your prospects in the top of the funnel and expect a certain percentage to convert into a lead or sale. This percentage is referred to as the conversion rate. The rate at which prospects become clients. There are things you can do to your website that can drastically Improve your conversion rate.

Working at the shoe store, we had to learn some tough web site usability lessons. We created a website which sold New Balance Shoes based on which foot problem you had. We couldn't compete on broad keywords such as "running shoes" because retail giants, like Nike, Reebok and Adidas were doing their best to keep us all on the second and third page of Google.

Our answer was to create landing pages about common foot problems. Morton's Neuroma, Plantar Fasciitis, Plantar Warts, Shoes for Diabetics... There were about twenty diagnoses that we targeted. A consumer would leave the podiatrist with a funky foot diagnosis and start searching on Google for a solution.

As soon as they searched for keyword phrases such as "plantar fasciitis shoes" our site would come right up.

You would first choose your foot problem, then indicate your gender, and finally, your desired activity, choosing between Running, Walking, Cross Training, or Tennis. Once selected, we would show you the three or four shoe styles that we recommended for you.

The system was quite successful. Annually, we sold more than half a million dollars' worth of shoes for foot problems for several years. Shockingly our conversion rate was only 1.5 percent.

Meaning, for everyone hundred visitors to the site, one and a half purchases occurred. We continued to challenge ourselves to achieve a two percent conversion rate. A very small increase as a percentage would mean huge increases in revenue.

We set out to do just that. We purchased the book; "Don't Make Me Think - A commonsense approach to web usability" by Steve Krug. Steve highlighted common sense marketing approaches that were commonly deployed around us all. For example, why is candy placed at the grocery store checkout? Why are department stores laid out in a certain way? We are being directed and guided constantly, without our awareness, for the most part.

With these real-world examples, Steve provided excellent insights on how your website should be displayed. More importantly, he demonstrated how to guide your visitors to take advantage of your calls to action.

We immediately deployed a few surprisingly basic adjustments. Right away, our conversion rate went up. We added the ability to add on accessory items such as insoles. Soon after, every third purchase included an insole upgrade. Better yet, insoles and other accessories yield a higher profit margin. We added automated questionnaires and automated responses to help customers find the shoes they needed for their foot problems. Better yet, we now could add many more people to our email list.

We removed clutter such as social media icons that were taking up highly valued real estate on our pages. It took some rethinking to get back to basics. When you're browsing the internet trying to figure out what you would like your site to look like, remember the basics. Get away from flashy animation, never-ending carousels, and pretty icons. Get back to the tried and true methods that have worked for decades. Many of these concepts predate the internet itself.

Getting Your Funnel Ready for Conversion

Phone Numbers

Place your phone number on the top and bottom of every page. A phone call is the best action a visitor make when visiting your website. The conversion rate of a phone call is almost always going to be higher than a contact form submission.

Calls to Action

On your website, place your logo on the top left and your strongest call to action on the top right. Adding a phone number that can be clicked on when using a cell phone is always a good practice.

Examples of Calls to Action

- Free Estimates, Call Now
- View Specials
- Sign Up for Savings
- Attend our Signature Event
- Create a Free Account

The Three Second Rule

The average visitor needs be directed and understand what you do next on your website within three seconds of visiting. Commonly the only things seen at first glance are above the fold or before you scroll.

If everything is in the proper place, your logo, your strong call to action in the top right corner, and your hero image with a strong call to action.

You Will Lose If

- Your logo does not match your industry or lend a clue as to what your company does.
- If the name of your company does not lend a clue as to what product and services you provide…
- If your marketing message is vague or unclear…

Keep them on Your Site

Place social media icons on the bottom of your site. Now that you have a visitor in your funnel, you do not want them leaving. Especially if you paid for a boosted Facebook ad or a paid Google ad. Instead, use that call to action area to sell something.

Contact Forms On Every Page

Making sure there is a "Quick Contact Form" on every page is important. Quick meaning only ask for the basics such as their name, phone number, and email address. Too many fields on a form can turn off the user.

Pro Tip: Adding a Call to Action at the top and bottom of every page increases conversion rates.

Example #1
The Roof Guy Annapolis Home Page

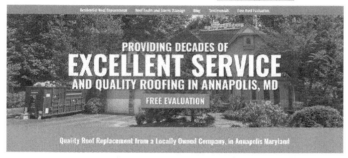

Quality Roof Replacement   Roof Repairs   Rapid Response

Notice the Strong Call to Action in the upper right. Also, note the Strong Call to Action in the main hero image. The industry is moving away from multiple slides because of usability and load times. Within seconds it is very clear what services The Roof Guy offers and what type of customer he serves.

Example #2
The Roof Guy Annapolis Landing Page

Residential Roof Replacement   Roof Leaks and Storm Damage   Blog   Testimonials   Free Roof Evaluation

Wind Damage to Your Roof and How to Detect It

Home » Roof Repairs » Wind Damage to Your Roof and How to Detect It

Wind Damage to Your Roof and How to Detect It

Here in the Chesapeake region, we have our fair share of extremely windy days. The issue is further compounded by intense summer storms and wintery nor'easters. Did you know the effects of the wind alone on your roof can be especially harmful? This is because the wind does not move uniformly over the surface. Specific areas are more vulnerable and suffer more significant damage. And, what's worse is that these effects are many times undetectable through a visual inspection from the ground. According to the National Roofing Contractors Association (NRCA), the most damage occurs at the edges. Furthermore, this type of damage starts out minimal and continues to grow if left unchecked. Once a corner is left exposed, rain can seep in and cause serious problems.

Here are signs to look out for wind damage to your roof and the reasons you need to fix it ASAP.

FREE EVALUATION

*Name

*Phone

*Email

Submit

RECENT BLOG POSTS

Recent Posts

No social media icons on the top of the site. We pushed them all to the bottom. On this landing page, you can see that we have included a contact form with an additional strong Call to Action. Open, clean white space, simple design, with obvious direction. Remember, most sales are closed over the phone.

Getting them from online to on-the-line is the key to a high close rate.

Your Website is Ready, Now What?

You now need the traffic to convert. What are your potential customers searching for, and how do they find you? Most in our local markets use Google and Facebook to seek out and find information. In a world of endless options, we recommend that you focus on the long-term investment of Google and use Facebook as a tool to drive immediate traffic to your website.

"There are only two ways to get traffic to your website, BUILD IT, or BUY IT!" ~ Lisa Cruz of Reach Local.

Chapter 11
What Does Google Want?

A MANUAL
OCTOBER 2015
160 PAGE MANUAL
HARD WORK + HONESTY
E.A.T & Y.M.O.Y.L.

CONTENT
GOOGLE CHECKS 1X PER MONTH
HATES SEEING THE SAME RERUNS
NEW, UP-TO-DATE INFORMATION
BE A GREAT RESULT!

POPULARITY
GOOD SITES LINK TO YOU,
YOU MUST BE POPULAR!
BAD SITES LINK TO YOU,
YOU MUST BE A BAD RESULT!

Let's put a little personality behind Google. What does Google want? Google wants to keep people using its search engine. For that to happen, good search results are a must. So, in turn, Google wants you to be a great result for their customers, the searchers. Becoming a consistent and trustworthy source of good results is the best way to grow your monthly search traffic.

The Manual - Just the Facts Ma'am!

In October 2015, Google released a one hundred sixty page manual for all to see. It gave some direction as to what Google was looking for and included some guidelines for best practices. To summarize, those who work hard and are honest will be rewarded with higher rankings.

For years tinkerers and hackers have been trying to cheat the system. These bad guys have been trying to rank higher regardless of the website's value, the messaging, or what was being forced onto the searcher. These sites would not only have bad content but often they would try to install malicious malware or dupe the unsuspecting browser. Google has been in a constant battle with these cheaters since the very beginning.

At one time, there was a high value on keywords and meta tags. This only lasted until the cheaters stuffed paragraphs and overused keywords trying to get a ranking. They showed a lack of concern for the quality of content or the user's experience. Now Google barely looks at metadata. Often, Google only notices when someone is trying to cheat the algorithm.

After this came an era when it was rumored that websites with the most links were considered the tops. Instantly, people were going link crazy. Sites were popping up just to sell links. Overnight, directory websites were scraping the internet just to farm out links. The ugliest is when computer programs called robots or "bots" spammed all of the blog comment sections. This caused most bloggers at the height of blogging to turn off the ability to comment on their posts. Once again, Google had to step in. Google now punishes sites that have these low-value inbound links. Be careful who you let link to you.

Recently, content quality was under the gun. Content was officially crowned the King of search engine optimization. Many people try to take the least expensive route, opting for less expensive offshore content creation, or allowing a novice writer to create or curate their copy. This could be their assistant, your high school daughter, or a neighborhood college student... not an expert in your field. This low-quality content was littering the internet. Before things got too far out of control, Google came out with two crucial content guidelines, which I've illustrated below.

E.A.T. = Expertise, Authority, Trustworthiness!

Google wants expert content! Not something you let your niece write because she needs the practice, and certainly not something written by someone from another country. Many undervalue how important it is to write the content themselves or hire a high-quality copywriter, or at times, both. If you know that writing is not your strength, don't waste time creating copy or content you know is below par. Your website and your marketing efforts deserve better.

Other indicators graded are readership level, copy length, topic, keywords, and a few more formatting best practices. Google can tell. How? Because they are comparing your site to every other site on the world wide web. By using various indicators, Google can spot what quality is and what is of little value to searchers.

Y.M.O.Y.L = Your Money or Your Life!

As drastic as this sounds, Google is sick and tired of its customers getting scammed by internet fraudsters. Now, and more in the future, Google will be taking a hard look at any website that offers content or sells products that will directly affect the wellbeing of the searchers.

- Think bad medical advice.
- Think online shopping scams.
- Think bad investment opportunities.
- Think Fake News!
- Be Unique or Be Left Out

O.P.C. Other People's Content

The same seven words in a row on two sites is a major red flag. Duplicate content is considered the cardinal search sin. Is your content authentic and one of a kind? Check for yourself. There are several online sites that you can use to verify that your copy is unique and original. Copyscape is the industry standard, easy to use, and very affordable. Copy and paste in a few of the paragraphs from your site. Just like Google, these engines can scan the web and tell you every instance, the date and the origin of the content. Google can do the same with photos too. So original photography counts! This practice is worth the effort if you're concerned about featuring in search engine results and protecting your online integrity.

New Episodes or Just a Bunch of Reruns?

Google gets so bored! Google scans the internet and looks at each website about once per month. Imagine, some of these websites have not changed in years. It would be like watching the same reruns of old episodes over and over again. Extremely dull... very unexciting.

When Google comes by your website and sees that you have new content and photos, it is very much like releasing a new episode. With excitement, Google notes your changes and can't wait to see more! A new article or blog post is all it takes to keep Google happy. In fact, with continued updates, Google will begin to favor your site and start coming by more often to check your new content. Better yet, this increased interest means your pages are being indexed in search more often, and your content is ranking higher.

Compare two local mechanics in your town. Mechanic A hasn't updated their website in almost ten years. Boring! On the other side of town, Mechanic B has been updating their site every month with how-to articles and being helpful by advising those searching for vehicle maintenance tips. Which website do you think Google will rank higher? A or B?

The answer, of course, is B. Google believes that a website that updates regularly, with new, fresh content is often a better search result, versus an old stagnant website. Your website needs to become a better result. Better than your competitors. Create good content at least once a month, and you will be rewarded with higher rankings in Google searches.

Content Pages vs. Home Pages

Each page of content that you create on your site can be found in a search. Google prefers to direct it's audience to a specific landing page, blog, product, or service page, rather than the Home Page. Google knows that it can save the user a click or two by guiding them directly to the page with the specific information they seek.

Search, "Sears Dishwasher." Google search results guide you right into the dishwasher section. Not the Sears Home Page. The Home Page is nowhere to be found, even after several pages of search results. Google doesn't want to risk the searcher getting lost or off track by starting them at the Sears Home Page. Google knows that searchers have a better chance of finding their desired result by directing them to a Landing Page instead of the Home Page.

Example #1
Keyword: "Fuel Tank Maintenance"

fuel polishing maryland

Dr. Fuel Clean - The Cure for Diesel Engines
https://www.drfuel.com/ ▾
Removal of Diesel Fuel Contaminants. · Clean & Polish Diesel Fuel. · **Fuel Polishing** System Installation.
· Gasoline Extraction & Disposal. · Click to Learn More!
Marine Pleasure Craft · Clean Fuel Blog · About Us · Contact Us Today

Marine Vehicle Fuel Tank Cleaning Services in Maryland
https://www.cleanfuelsassociates.com/index.php?sub_folder=1&page...fuel... ▾
As time went by more and more benefits were discovered with updated **fuel polishing** methods such as
Ethanol removal and preventing the reduction of gasoline ...

Fuel Polishing & Filtration Services - Clean Fuels Associates
https://www.cleanfuelsassociates.com/commercial-fuel.../fuel-filtration-services.html ▾
Clean Fuels Associates is an industry leader when it comes to **fuel polishing** and filtration services for
fuel-based businesses in **Maryland** and along the Eastern ...

Brads Fuel Filtering: Home
https://bradsfuelfiltering.com/ ▾
Brad's **Fuel** Filtering Inc. 3515 Marmenco Ct Baltimore, MD 21230. Office: 410.834.5000. Copyrights ©
2018 Brad's **Fuel** Filtering. All rights reserved.
Fuel Contamination · Free Fuel Test · Brad's Filtration Process · Chemicals

USA Fuel Service — Tilghman Oil Company
https://www.tilghmanoil.com/services-2/usa-fuel-service/ ▾
USA Fuel Service, LLC is one of the nation's largest professional **fuel polishing**/tank cleaning companies
and fuel additive producers. We provide complete ...

Fuel Polishing Southern Maryland - The Hull Truth - Boating and ...
https://www.thehulltruth.com › ... › Mid Atlantic and Chesapeake Bay ▾
Aug 3, 2014 - 3 posts - 3 authors
Mid Atlantic and Chesapeake Bay - **Fuel Polishing** Southern **Maryland** - Anyone know of a service down
this way?

Notice that Clean Fuels ranked 2nd and 3rd for "Fuel Polishing Maryland." Neither page ranked is the Home Page. Each of these product and service pages bring new customers to the Clean Fuels website each month.

Example #2
Keyword: "Chesapeake Bay Fishing Report"

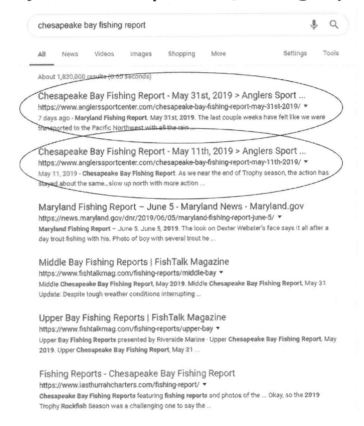

Notice that Angler's ranks 2nd and 3rd under the State of Maryland for "Chesapeake Bay fishing report." Neither page ranked is the Home Page. The blog ranked second, and a specific fishing report ranked 3rd. These posts bring huge amounts of traffic to the site month over month. Sometimes there will even be a third post ranked in the top 5.

More, Quality Content = More Monthly Traffic

Each page you put out on the internet is another opportunity to gain more visitors through search. Do not think of your content as "here today and gone tomorrow." Google is not Facebook, Snapchat, or any other Insta-gratification social media site. When it comes to search results, you need to change your ideas about content. Each page will continue to be found in search month after month until it is removed from the internet.

Example #3
Denise Dental Studio Annapolis

POPULAR PAGES
PAGE VIEWS

PAGE	PAGE VIEWS	AVG. TIME ON PAGE	ENTRANCES
/abscessed-tooth-causes-symptoms-treatment/			+211.57% 377 vs 121
/worry-toothache-serious/			+282.28% 302 vs 79
/what-is-the-difference-between-regular-x-rays-digital-and-3-d-x-rays/			+147.13% 215 vs 87
/			+50.51% 149 vs 99
/old-silver-amalgam-fillings-need-replaced/			+100.00% 118 vs 59
/grinding-clinching-really-need-night-guard/			+162.50% 105 vs 40
/dos-donts-brushing-teeth/			+108.33% 50 vs 24

Denise Dental Studio was reaping the benefits of consistently blogging for several months in a row. In the graphic above, you can see the number of entrances to the site. Three of the top landing pages had more entrances than the Homepage. These landing pages generate this organic traffic month in and month out. The more quality content placed on the website, the more the monthly traffic builds. For every one hundred visitors, a certain percentage will call and become new clients. Therefore, you need to invest in quality content.

Consistently contributing quality content will organically grow a website's monthly traffic. Directing and converting visitors into sales is the true definition of Search Engine Optimization. Especially in an environment where Artificial Intelligence is automatically generating real-time results based on your search history, location history, GPS coordinates, and social media habits.

Much like a bell curve, as a website is recognized by Google to be a provider of high-quality content, like a tide, all rankings for related keywords will rise.

Is Your Link Game Strong?

This last part couldn't be more simple and at the same time complex. As we mentioned before, in a not so distant past, it was rumored that Google ranked websites by the number of websites linking to them. The abuse was rampant, and an update was implemented. Today, the quality of a link plus quantity of links both to other websites and from a website affect how Google decides.

Sound Complex? Allow Us to Simplify

If popular, and local websites link to your website, your site must be popular. Google loves these types of earned or natural links.

If unpopular sites link to your site, you must be unpopular. Such as spammy blogs or link farm directories. Submitted or purchased links are frowned upon heavily.

A website must be a genuine effort to inform, educate, and provide value in order to be ranked well by Google. Honesty, good content, hard work, and quality win.

Chapter 12
Back to Build it or Buy It

Getting Social

Use social media, but be in control of your sales funnel. When boosting posts on Social Media, ALWAYS LINK BACK TO YOUR LANDING PAGES! All of those likes and shares DO VERY LITTLE to get visitors to your sales funnel. Linking back to your content is crucial to controlling the environment and promoting a higher conversion rate.

You've installed proven conversion elements. You have Strong Calls to Action, and you have Quick Contact Forms on every page. You have tested your site, and you know your conversion rates. Your site is the best place for your customers. You've made sure of it. That's why you need to get prospects to your controlled environment. No reputable expert has ever been able to pin down the value of a Like or a Share. On the flip side, by using simple math, a website can be evaluated for performance.

Pay to Play

Facebook is a bold-faced liar. They've created a confusing environment for the everyday consumer. They've told everyone that they needed to gather Likes and promote business on "pages" instead of promoting one's personal brand on a "profile."

Then after going public on the stock market, they drastically reduced the visibility of non-paid posts by up to eighty-five to ninety percent. Introducing "boosting" as the new way to pay to play and promoting it as the only way to connect with your "Likes."

On the positive side, Facebook did introduce the ability to target strangers. But, this is now done for a price. In a hyper-local networking arena, utilizing your personal profile to promote your personal brand will generate far more reach. Sounds simple, right?

Currently, Facebook is the King of social media and if you do not pay Facebook, they limit how many people see your posts. Even if you have one thousand likes on your Facebook Page, only ten-fifteen percent may ever see your posts unless you boost them. Boosting posts that link back to your content is a wonderful way to fill your Sales Funnel.

Boost Your Way to Success

Go ahead, click the Boost Post button. Play around with the demographics and targeting. The choices are endless.

Facebook now gives users the ability to not only pick what users are interested in or "like," but also specific demographics and purchasing habits. You can pick "business owners only," "homeowners only," "recent homeowners", or "Facebook Page Administrators" to highlight a few. The options and combinations seem endless.

You can place your content right in front of the perfect audience and send quality visitors back to your website to convert. Right now, the Facebook ads cost a fraction of Google Adwords.

A Social Media Click vs. A Google Search Click

Like comparing apples to oranges, the mindset and intent of the two different audiences differ greatly. When you're using social media, the intent is to attract an audience by engaging. Remain present and create an impulse decision. Often direct offers do not convert well in a social media environment. Smart marketing companies are directing social media traffic to landing pages to move prospects further along in the sales funnel.

Traffic from Google is much different. Typically, when someone is searching on Google, they are searching for a solution to a problem. Often, these problems include a wallet waving in the air to fan the flames of that day's fire. Google organic visitors and Google paid ad visitors have a much more aggressive intent; to attempt to solve the problem themselves or to call in an expert. The number of conversions and the rate of conversion is often a little better, more predictable, and consistent.

Buying Google Ads

With billions of clicks already recorded across all industries, Google can tell you what to expect. Meaning, you are not the first one in your industry to try Google Ads.

Google has hundreds, if not thousands, of industry examples to use to predict accurate estimations of results. Google uses industry demographics, local demographics, location, and the monthly budget to determine the possible outcomes. With accuracy, Google can estimate how many calls you will get and how much each call will cost. Google Ads have decades of proven success, especially if you are driving the traffic back to a website with a high conversion rate. If the website is out of date and lacks clear calls to action, the cost per conversion can be abnormally high.

The Costs of Buying Google Ads

It is each business owner's responsibility to understand their numbers and know how much they can afford to pay for client acquisition. It's important to realize the value of that client over a lifetime and so on.

Here are examples of two catering companies in the same town. Both companies are looking to grow their sales.

First, we took all of the gross revenue from the previous year and divided it by how many jobs they had completed. The average of each catering job for Catering Company A was $3,000.00. Google estimated that it would cost $50 per phone call. When asked, the sales team said they could close half of the calls. Reminding them that these would be colder leads in some cases, they adjusted their estimate to one in five or twenty percent. If each call costs $50, and it takes five calls to complete a sale, then the costs per client acquisition is $250. The client was happy to pay $250 for a $3,000.00 catering job.

On the other hand, Catering Company B has an average gross sale of $750. Suddenly, $250 does not make sense. Giving up thirty-three percent in ad costs is leaving no room for profit. So, make sure you know your cost per client numbers in and out.

Chapter 13
Creating Useful Content

What's The Point of Blogging Anyway?

You've heard that you need to be blogging, but why? They say it is hard to get motivated when you do not know what the result will bring. We all know success rates plummet without planning and motivation. You are about to spend a considerable amount of time and effort "blogging," so there better be a game plan!

Here is a recap of the benefits of consistent content building.

Google Search Traffic

You are creating pages that will be listed in Google's Search Results. When you search for a keyword, Google attempts to connect you with a "Landing Page" not a Homepage. Why would they do this? In a well-calculated effort, Google is attempting to connect the searcher with a better result and experience. Imagine yourself searching [dishwashers at Sears]. Google painstakingly selects the best pages within Sears' website to display. Results 1-8 are Sear's dishwasher pages from within their site. The Sears Home Page is in the 9th position of Google's results. This means is that you can expect many more visitors to come from your posts and pages than your Homepage.

Better Customer Experience

Blogging creates focused "landing pages" for your website. A better user experience will lead to better results. If you direct your audience to the specific information they seek, your chances of conversion drastically increase. Reduce the number of clicks the user needs to take, keep your calls to action clear and your marketing message simple. This will lead to improved results.

Branding Reinforcement

Engaging and connecting with the existing audience you've invested a considerable amount of time and effort to build your client base and circle of influence. Now, more than ever, you cannot afford to let it all fizzle out. Reminder Marketing has been used for ages to reinforce a brand within its own community.

Think about Coke and Pepsi. You either love one or the other. You have decided long ago which taste you like and which brand you favor. So why did Coca Cola spend more than $4,000,000,000 (four billion dollars) on marketing in 2016? To remind you of how thirsty you are. Even deeper, seeing an advertisement for your favorite food or beverage will trigger something within, making you feel hungry or thirsty even when you were not before.

More Traffic

Feeding your Online Sales Funnel. To generate new traffic, you are going to need new content. As mentioned, good articles come up in search and draw in new potential clients to your online sales funnel. For every one hundred visitors, there should be a result. Generating new pages will help get your web site's traffic from zero to several hundred visitors each month and beyond.

Great for Social Media and Email

Content makes great fodder for your marketing cannon. What do you plan to send out in your weekly or monthly newsletter? What do you plan on posting to Social Media? Great content is the perfect place for your visitors to land. Make sure to design your emails and social media posts to drive traffic back to your website. Your website is the best place for your potential clients. Getting them away from social media, or their email inboxes is the best way to get their undivided attention.

Writer's Block Anyone?

Not all of us feel so creative. Writing about our products and services may not have been part of the original business plan, and certainly wasn't part of the traditional marketing plan you envisioned. Ads and Coupons are now seen as wallpaper and publication after publication using these means continue to go out of business. Today, we must make connections and evoke emotions to earn the attention of our prospects.

So, what are you going to write about? I hate to answer with, "it depends," but it will vary from business to business.

As we look at a few examples, it is important to put yourself in your client's shoes. Walk a mile or two in them. What troubles them? What are their professional or personal hardships? How can you help them? How can you educate them? How can you gain their trust? What are they wondering about?

Mind Mapping is a great brainstorming technique that could be used to come up with some ideas.

Let's look at a few topic examples from common industries we engage with while Networking.

Real Estate Agents

- How to Stage Your Home for Sale
- 10 Steps to Prepping Your Home for Market
- Buying a Home 101
- How to Sell Your Home Without an Agent
- This Year's Market Predictions

Photographers

- Step up Your Cell Phone Photography
- Where Not to Have Your Photos Printed
- 3 Steps to Taking a Great Family Photo

- Family Photo Home Décor Tips
- Safekeeping Your Family's Memories

Trainers and Coaches

- 5 Ways to Ask for That Promotion
- How to Advance in Today's Job Market
- 10 Habits Successful Business People Have
- How to Avoid a Mid-Career Crisis

What's the game plan here? I mean, are we telling photographers to give out free photography lessons to their prospects? Why? What could a photographer gain by giving away this type of information for free?

Be the Expert

Showing your craft to others allows them to get more engaged with your business. They will get to know some of the ins and outs of your process. Understanding this could give them a whole new respect for your profession. Especially your pricing. Now that you placed yourself in the position of teaching, you have given yourself a platform from which to promote yourself.

The Givers Gain. Books have been written about how being generous creates relationships and helps you gain trust within your market. Imagine the photographer giving a few free workshops or private lessons to someone who has some shred of interest.

He or she is going to ask you those questions that usually come up when someone advances their skills to the next level. You are now continuing the conversation. You are allowing the person to naturally find their talent ceilings or interest levels. You've helped them enhance their day-to-day lives, but when it comes to getting professional photography done, they will ask the one who's been the most helpful.

The same goes for referrals. If you demonstrate that you are the local expert and give away bits and pieces of your information, your name is most likely to be mentioned when someone is seeking your talents and skills.

Use Pictures to Tell Your Story

We think in colors and images; therefore, it is very important to add an image to your new content. Finding the right image is no easy task. With millions of copyright-free stock images, it is easy to come off cheap and unprofessional. We wouldn't want to use "clip art" now that we are professionals.

Subscribe to Adobe Stock, Thinkstock, IStockPhoto, Getty Images, or another national image subscription service. Canva is also a popular choice for those just getting started. Look for images that evoke emotions. If your topic is addressing a pain point in your prospect's life, support that with a matching photo. Another good image would show what it looked like after a prospect uses your services to solve their problem.

Make it Snappy

Try not to overdo it. There is no need to write a book every time you start blogging. Now more than ever before, people don't have the time to read a long post. A quick two to four-minute read is the perfect amount of information for our on-the-go lifestyles.

An informative three to five paragraphs will do just fine. You can even give a hint to the reader as to how long the post is, by the way, it's titled. You may have noticed the ever-popular list titles. As an example, "5 ways to write a great blog", or "3 things you don't want to miss when blogging". These "Listicle" titles are meant to signal to the end user that the information can be consumed quickly. They entice the consumer to abandon their Facebook feeds, or inboxes, for just a few moments to absorb your carefully crafted information.

If you feel that you have a subject that needs a deeper look, why not break it up into a series? That way, you give yourself that many more opportunities to distribute new content to your circle of influence.

Don't Reinvent the Wheel

Before you write your content, go right to Google to observe how others have written before you. Google your topic and start to look at the sites listed in the top ten search results. Examine their writing styles and content. Please take note that Google thinks these are the best results possible. If Google grades these posts and pages as the best, then you should try to match the efforts of these pages. Use these pages as a guide or outline as to how you are going to write your post. Take note of their length, reading level, and subtopics.

Sprinkle in a Touch of Local

Google loves local, and sprinkling in some local keywords or locations will go a long way towards getting you found online. Google is constantly trying to match users to the best results, and a primary factor is a location. As we walk around with our smartphones, Google is keeping tabs of our location history.

That way if we search for "best food near me," Google can give us a local result we can rely on. Even if you search "best food," Google will look at your location and give you a local result. Local search results are always primary, and global or national search results are secondary. It has been this way for several years and was done to lend a better end user experience. We used to have to search for "best food in Annapolis, MD" to find a local result. This is no longer the case.

What to Do After You Post

You have written and published your post, now what? Remember why we posted in the first place. We needed to spread the word about our business but didn't have anything to say. Now that we have some content let's spread the word.

Head to Social Media and start posting a link back to your Landing Page.

Spread Your Message on Social Media

Remember the object is to get users away from Facebook's' sales funnel and into your sales funnel. Facebook is not in love with this idea, and that is one of the reasons you are going to have to pay to boost your posts. Boosting your posts will get your message in front of not only your audience but a new targeted audience as well. As Facebook continues to be pressured by stockholders, we are headed for a day where if you do not pay, your posts will no longer be seen by your audience.

Send an Email to Your Fans

Craft an email to be sent to your lists. Keep in mind that we want our prospects to leave their inboxes and go to your sales funnel. Meaning, only include a synopsis of your post with a large read more button. This way, if the prospect wants the meat and potatoes, they will have to visit your website to read the entire post.

Posting to social media and emailing your list should drive traffic to your sales funnel. The result will be new phone calls, new sign ups, and new emails. For every one hundred visitors, a percentage will convert.

Workshop 13.1
Creating Useful Content

Brainstorming Topics

What problems do every one of your clients complain about? What do they hate about your industry? What are the stereotypes? What are the problems you have solutions for? People make choices based on pain and pleasure.

List five problems or complaints you often hear from your prospects.

1.

2.

3.

4.

5.

Find a Clever Title

To get the attention of a prospect an engaging title is a must. The title will need to convince the reader that the content can solve a problem in a short amount of time, or the content can help the reader avoid a disaster.

Use one of these title formulas to create engaging titles.

- How to [fill in the blank] without [fill in the blank].

- How to get in front of your customers without wasting your marketing budget.

Another...

- [Fill in the blank] simple steps for [fill in the blank].

- 4 simple steps for getting found online.

More Templates

Here is an impressive list of templates from Elizabeta Perstneva of SEMRush.

Keep it Simple
- #____Tips
- ____ vs ____
- # Bad ____ Habits
- ____ Facts and Myths
- # Ways to ____

Offer useful information.
- What everyone out to know about ____
- Little Know Ways to ____
- A Cheat Sheet for ____
- The Ultimate Guide to ____
- ____: The Ultimate Checklist

Use "How", "Why" or "What"
- Where to Find____
- How to ____ Like a Pro/Boss
- What to do with ____
- How to ____ That Drives ____

Create a Sense of Urgency
- How to Rock ____
- How to ____ in ____ Easy Steps

- ____ Quick ____ Tips
- The Real Truth about ____
- The Secret of Successful ____

Overpromise!
- To World Cheapest/Best/Worst
- The # Deadly Sins of ____
- # Essential Steps to ____
- # Killer Strategies to ____

Fill in the Body

Now that you have a title in mind try to list three or more ways that your product and service helps solve the problem (pain or pleasure).

1.

2.

3.

Other questions to consider. Will you have an offer? What are the offer details? Is there an upcoming Holiday that you can tie into your
promotion? Do you have a special event coming up or could you plan one?

Close with a Call to Action

Always end with a call to action. Not a hard sell, but a request to inquire more, to join the conversation or attend an event.

Can't Bring Yourself to Write?

Hire someone competent to write for you. Ask for references if you don't know any content writers. Whether you are doing your own writing or hiring a writer, you need to understand how your content should be structured.

Distribution

Now that you have an article written and a graphic selected, it is time to distribute your message to the masses.

Get Social - Use social media as an inexpensive way to advertise. Facebook boosts are drastically cheaper than Google Adwords, or most traditional print media. Select your audience, choose how many days you want your post to circulate, and boost the post.

Email is still #1 - Look at email addresses as the most valuable marketing asset you can collect. Send a small excerpt of your post to your email lists. Remember to make sure that if they want to read the entire post, they must visit your website. Keep your emails brief and to the point. Do not clutter up your message. Remember, everyone you meet during networking goes on an email list.

Print it out! - Why not convert your article into a flyer or hand out for your next networking event? Stand out by handing out valuable information rather than just your business card.

Chapter 14
Too Many Social Media Options

With so many social media options and platforms available today, how should you go about deciding where and how to post? It's probably not a good idea to post to all of them. You should be more targeted and strategic. There are several factors to consider.

One factor is the type of business you have. A marketing company can benefit from showing great graphics on a visually based platform like Instagram or Snapchat. A business that is best represented by words will do well on Linkedin or Reddit.

Arguably the most important thing to consider is your target audience. If you are primarily hoping to appeal to women, Pinterest may be a great platform choice. You'll find a younger audience on Snapchat or Instagram.

The final consideration would be the platform itself. I've outlined all the particulars about each platform below. Take a minute to review this information and consider the question at the end of the selection. Decide if this platform is right for your business and your audience.

Twitter

Once a giant and still a top player in the social media universe, Twitter has grown to 330 million users. Results seem to be spotty though, with some having success and others not. It is my opinion that without the 2016 presidential election, Twitter would have fallen off the branch. But, with now President Trump constantly creating newsworthy tweets, the brand had a semi-successful resurgence. Election meddling investigations revealed that approximately a quarter of the user accounts are fake, and seven percent are computer programs called bots.

Twitter does have its strengths. First, you can advertise so that you can reach a targeted audience.

Twitter is Google friendly, so tweets and content come up in search. You can send a direct message to someone which often stands out in a sea of emails. Want a little better reach on Twitter? Make sure to include a photo. Tweets with photos get an eighteen percent higher click-thru rating, approximately ninety percent more likes, and three times the retweets.

Twitter Stats
- 330M Active
- 50/50, Some have success, others not so much
- One in four accounts is fake
- Seven percent of the 330M are robots
- It's an effective way to send a message or receive one
- You can advertise
- Tweets with images get eighteen percent higher CTR, eighty-nine percent more likes, and three times more retweets
- Good for Search Engine Optimization (SEO)

On a scale of 1-5 (5 being the best), how important is Twitter for your audience?   _____

Instagram

Purchased by Facebook, Instagram is an ever-growing presence. Users who use Instagram, log in often. The platform has over 800M active users with over 500M logging in every day. Pay close attention to the demographics. Sixty-eight percent of users are female, with most being eighteen to twenty-nine years old. Companies are getting onboard too.

Approximately 25M businesses are using Instagram, and that number is growing. You can advertise on Instagram and pick out your target audiences. Don't have an Instagram profile currently? No worries, you can still advertise through the Facebook Ads Manager. If you do not advertise, it is a bit difficult to get users back to your landing pages. Clicking on a post does not activate a link. Most drop a link in the post or profile description which is not ideal for click throughs. Hashtags work very well on Instagram, increasing engagement by over ten percent. You can follow specific hashtags in your news feed. Instagram is a great opportunity to post a video or photo.

Instagram Stats
- 800M Active
- 500M Active daily users and growing quickly with 25M Businesses having Instagram profiles

- You can advertise through your Facebook Ads Manager
- Sixty-eight percent of users are female, fifty-nine percent of users are eighteen to twenty-nine, and thirty-three percent of users are thirty to forty-nine years old
- #Hashtags work and increase engagement by 12.6 percent
- Great opportunity to post a video or photo
- Not good for referral traffic to your website

On a scale of one to five (five being the best), how important is Instagram to your brand? _____

Pinterest

By far, women pin the most. Pinterest is a wonderful place to find positive inspiration. Whether it is ideas for recipes, decorating, or throwing the best party, over 175M people use Pinterest with four-fifths being women, most over the age of forty. Millennial women are starting to use Pinterest as much as Instagram, logging on several times per day. When polled, a majority said that they had made purchases based on pins. Often Pinterest is a source of research before purchase. With pins directly linking to landing pages, Pinterest is an excellent source of online referral traffic. A visual experience, Pinterest is a great place to post photos.

Pinterest Stats
- 175M Active Users
- Eighty-One percent of users are female
- Millennials use Pinterest as much as Instagram
- Eighty-Seven percent polled have made a purchase based off a pin
- Seventy percent of Pinners are over forty years old
- A major source for referral website traffic
- Wonderful place to post photos

On a scale of 1-5 (5 being the best), how important is Pinterest to your audience? _____

Reddit

The wild west of Social Media is Reddit. With over 250M active users, Reddit is an excellent place to consume news, blog posts, and photos. Topics are broken down into categories called Sub-Reddits. Within the over 800k categories, posts are voted up and down, and comments can be ruthless. Being disingenuous or not following the rules of the Sub-Reddits is frowned upon. Over seventy percent of users are liberal men. Most are between the ages of eighteen to twenty-nine.

Reddit Stats
- 250M Active
- Great for News, Blog Posts, and Photos
- Seventy-eight percent primarily use for news
- Seventy-one percent Male
- Fifty-nine percent are eighteen to twenty-nine years old
- Topics are categorized into /Subs
- There are 853,000 Subs
- The community votes posts up or down
- Comments are allowed but monitored
- Great for referral traffic

On a scale of 1-5 (5 being the best), how important is Reddit to your audience? _____

SnapChat

SnapChat continues to be the choice of Gen Y and Z. Most of the 300M users are under thirty-four years old. Half of these are between eighteen and twenty-four. But boy are they active. SnapChat may take the record for most times checked per day by users. Active users are logging more than eighteen times per day. The premise is that what you post publicly will disappear within twenty-four hours. There is also an incentive to post publicly daily and back and forth with your contacts, to keep your "trend going." Private messages are also supposed to disappear as well. With massive data breaches these days, this is a big plus for users.

SnapChat Stats
- 300M Active
- 178M Daily Active Accounts
- Thirty Min Avg Per Day
- Seventy-Four percent of users are under thirty-four years old
- Half of all users are eighteen to twenty-four
- Active users check eighteen times per day
- Thirty percent of all Millennials Snap

On a scale of 1-5 (5 being the best), how important is SnapChat to your audience? _____

YELP

An oldie but goodie... for some. At fourteen plus years old, YELP is one of the oldest companies on the web. With 145M visits a month, much of YELP's marketing spend is used to attract those visits. Mostly on mobile, and slightly more women than men, YELP's results are heavy into retail. Four categories make up four-fifths of all traffic; shopping, home services, food, and beauty/fitness. If you are not in one of those categories, there is very little reason to advertise with YELP. Not to mention, YELP requires long term contracts, and it is not easy to pin down a cost per conversion.

YELP Stats
- 145M Monthly Visits
- Thirty percent Desktop, Seventy percent Mobile
- 60/40 Female
- Ages twenty-five to forty-five
- Fifty-eight percent make +$50k annually
- Popular categories; Shopping, Home Services, Food, and Beauty & Fitness
- These categories make up seventy-eight percent of the monthly traffic
- Make sure to claim your business
- Advertising is expensive and has long contracts
- Yelp reviews can also help rankings in search engines

On a scale of 1-5 (5 being the best), how important is Yelp to your market? _____

LinkedIn

Forty percent of the world's millionaires have a LinkedIn profile. Most LinkedIn users earn more than the national average. LinkedIn is a tenth of the size of Facebook, and over seventy percent of the users are international. LinkedIn is a great place to look for prospects. You can search through your connections' contact list and look for specific industries.

This creates a great way to ask for warm introductions. Unfortunately, users do not log in often enough. The average person only spends seventeen minutes a month on LinkedIn. Other platforms such as Facebook, Instagram, and Snapchat are exceeding that time in one day.

When people are on LinkedIn, they are usually checking up on someone's background and work history. So, make sure that your profile is complete and looking elite.

LinkedIn Stats
- 250M Active

- Some B2B but not much
- Your Profile needs to be elite
- LinkedIn is a top source that people use to validate you after a meeting
- Great platform for messaging prospects
- Wonderful place to search for new prospects for warm introductions
- Seventy percent of users are international
- Forty percent of active users spend only seventeen minutes per month
- Forty-four percent of users make more than 75k per year
- Forty-one percent of Millionaires use LinkedIn

On a scale of 1-5 (5 being the best), how important is LinkedIn to your audience? _____

Facebook

The big dog! Hands down, Facebook is used the most. Facebook has faced several scandals in recent years and is most likely to weather several more storms in the future. For now and for the foreseeable future, the Social Media Giant is very present and not going anywhere anytime soon.

Facebook Stats
- 2,072M Active (or 2.072 Billion)
- 1.36B Daily desktop and 1.57B daily mobile users
- Split evenly, fifty-three percent are female, and forty-seven percent are male
- Sixty-three percent of people ages 50+ use Facebook
- Only five percent of the 50M small businesses boost posts
- Facebook reduces the visibility of your page posts by as much as ninety percent, forcing you to pay to play.
- The average user is connected to one hundred fifty friends, plus eighty pages, groups or events.
- Facebook is a great place to post blog posts, photos, and video. Photos and videos get more engagement.
- Leverage Facebook Live and Facebook Messenger to continue the conversation.

Facebook Profile

This is your personal feed. Your profile is used to access your groups and pages.

Facebook Business Page

Used by businesses, pages give you the ability to BOOST posts and reach new audiences.

Facebook Groups

A fantastic way to continue the conversation. Think subscription. Members will receive notifications, but you cannot boost.

Facebook Business Page Posts

- Rule#1 make sure your posts link back to your site.
- Rule #2 boost posts that link back to your site.
- No hashtags needed.

Facebook Videos

Video is so big on Facebook that they have launched a network. Facebook Live continues to get increased engagement. I'm not a huge fan of every video being a Live Video. If you record your videos you can not only edit them, you can upload them to multiple platforms.

Facebook Galleries

Posting photos is a wonderful way to get engagement and use little to no words. Facebook wants there to be less than twenty percent of the total space to contain text. The less text, the more people Facebook will show the image to.

Facebook Messenger

Use messenger to reach out and continue the conversation. It seems easier to continue the conversation or even start a conversation on Facebook Messenger... More comfortable than a warm email or text message. We never suggest sending cold messages.

Sending too many messages too frequently is frowned upon. Sending messages with links that cause the user to leave Facebook is frowned upon.

Facebook Events

Creating an event is a fantastic way to engage with interested users. Like a group, users get notified of updates. Like a post, you can boost.

Facebook Pixel

Install the code on your site so that Facebook can give you more insights. Pixel traffic can be tracked and re-targeted for additional marketing.

On a scale of 1-5 (5 being the best), how important is Facebook to your audience? _____

Google Users

Did you know you do not have to have a Gmail account to have a Google account? Even if you have an iPhone, you can still use Google. Having a Google account is crucial to successful local marketing. There are options such as Microsoft and Apple, but Google offers a full suite of functional software for today's entrepreneur. In fact, ninety-two percent of startups are using Gmail. And, if you want to take your company's data to the cloud, Google Files Stream (formally Google Drive) is a terrific option.

- +1.2B Active
- You do not have to have Gmail to create a Google account
- Google has free add-ons such as Docs, Drive, Gmail, Calendar, and tons more
- Ninety-two percent of startups use Gmail
- $5 per month per professional email
- Gmail works on iPhones
- Provides a free listing for all businesses on Google Maps
- Google Maps appears before organic results
- Google Adwords is a terrific way to buy traffic. The top 3 ads get forty percent of the clicks

YouTube

Millennials are swaying toward YouTube for their main source of content viewing. Zillennials are already there. One and two-year-old children can easily navigate children's programs on YouTube. YouTube is a giant, and one of the only real competitors of Facebook. They recently announced stories just like Facebook, Instagram, and Snapchat. You can now even go Live on YouTube. YouTube is going to be an increasingly important part of your success with local marketing.

YouTube Stats
- 1.3B Active
- 5B Videos watched each day, and by 2025 half of America's viewers will no longer subscribe to cable.

Google My Business

As we mentioned, you do not need a Gmail email address to sign up for a Google Account. Google My Business is where you set up your Map Listing and monitor your reviews. This is a crucial step to ensure people can find your business online.

- Add photos and confirm your map listing

- Provides search insights, map data, phone calls, and more
- Earn reviews
- Make sure to monitor and respond to each review
- Reviews help with SEO
- Respond positively to all the bad reviews

Google Search Console

A free and very powerful account. The Search Console is where you monitor the health of your website as it pertains to Google Search. This is the place to install your Site Map and check to make sure Google is reading your Robots.txt file. You can also request for Google to review your site and monitor any errors that may be preventing your from indexing in the search engine.

- Connect your website to GSC
- Submit a Site Map
- Verify your Robots.txt file
- "Fetch" the latest copy of your site

Google Analytics

A must-have! Google Analytics is free and powerful. See what seems like an unlimited amount of data sets for your website traffic. Which pages, what time, what operating systems? Measure cell phone versus desktop users and so much more. Create an account, and install the small code provided and tracking will begin.

Use this free service to track web traffic and visitor behavior.

On a scale of 1-5 (5 being the best), how important is Google to your business? _____

Chapter 15
Four Formulas to Measure Success

Often, we concern ourselves with the activities of marketing, but don't stop to evaluate and measure their effectiveness. If you don't measure success, how do you know you are achieving it? There are certain formulas you can use to check and see how your marketing is (or isn't) working for you.

Are you familiar with the term "floundering"? My Dad used to tell me I was floundering. I wasn't sure what he meant, but now as a fisherman, I understand the analogy. Think of a fish swimming in the water with direction. Now, think of a fish flopping around on the pier. That's what you're doing if you don't have a clear understanding of where you are and where you're going.

You can only flounder for so long. Soon, you will run out of air. This is what usually happens when people must give up on their dream, or at least put it on hold, while they go back to "work" to support themselves or their family.

Use these formulas to make sure you're staying on track with your marketing goals.

Website Conversion Rate
Conversions / Visitors = Conversion Rate

Your website receives one hundred visitors. Two of them called or emailed.

Your conversion rate is two percent.

2 conversions / 100 visitors = 2%

Pro Tip: The national average is one to three percent but with good strong calls to action you can reach results of ten to twenty percent.

Cost Per Conversion
Budget / Conversions = Cost Per Conversion

You boosted a post on Facebook for $100 which resulted in one hundred visits to your website. Each visit to your website cost $1.00. Two visitors called or emailed. The cost of each call or email was $50.

$100 / 2 conversions = $50 each

Close Rate
Number of Sales / Number of Prospects = Close Rate

Once in contact, how often does your prospect complete a purchase?

How many attempts does it take to complete a sale? four, ten, twenty? Let us use four in this example.

1 Sale / 4 Prospects = 25% Close Rate

Cost Per Sale Acquisition
Budget / Sale = Cost Per Sale Acquisition

$100 to create two Conversions. Each Conversion costs $50. It took four conversions (4 x $50 = $200) to get one Sale.

$200 / 1 Sale = $200 Cost Per Sale Acquisition

Chapter 16
Quotes from Main Street

"Entrepreneurs are #1 Open to Learn #2 Optimistic #3 Accountable." ~ Paul Riecks InSight.

Paul leads several professional peer groups in the Baltimore region. After interviewing hundreds of entrepreneurs over his career, Paul says that these are the three most prominent commonalities.

"Don't let the distractions become the attraction." ~ Casey Coven of Cruise Planners 411.

Casey, former president of the national professional women's group, ABWA, gave me this insightful advice. Are your distractions simple, like too much social media during the day? Are they complex, such as letting negativity drag you off course? Even worse, are you allowing yourself to be "productive" even though those actions don't help accomplish your ultimate goal? "Good" distractions are still distractions.

"Every prospect pays you." ~ Pat Voelkel.

A good friend Pat used to be a used car salesman. He would place a hundred dollar bill in his pocket. He knew he was going to face nineteen rejections before he was going to score with a sale. So he reminded himself each time a new customer pulled up on the lot by tapping his pocket. This action kept him in positive spirits, regardless of the outcome.

"Man plans, God laughs" ~ Donna Deter.

Donna introduced me to this quote, which is translated from Yiddish "Mann Tracht, Un Gott Lacht." WOW! No truer words have been spoken. You can plan and plan and plan... but until you put your ideas in motion, you can't know the reality. Almost every time, you will find that your plans will need to change and adjust to thrive. So, don't plan too far ahead or with too much detail because often you will need to change your plans anyway.

"If you're not happy, you better be telling me." ~ Ken Fischer of Fischer IT.

Ken tells each of his customers this when they start services. He sets a clear expectation and opens the door to allow the client to feel comfortable complaining. Better to complain to him than to his competition.

"When one door closes, two always open." ~ Random Voice on TV.

Isn't that true? Ever lose a job and think life was over? Then a few weeks later, you take a job even better than the one before. If you are positive, you will always find an opportunity.

Stephen Karpman's Drama Triangle - the Persecutor, the Victim, and the Rescuer.

In almost every conflict, characters take their roles. Then quickly fight to change their positions. The more roles change, the more drama ensues. Please take the time to look this one up online and read more.

"W.A.I.T. = Why Am I Talking." ~ David Wendkos of Sandler Training.

David, a certified Sandler Trainer, was a talker, just like myself. He often found himself talking the most in a conversation. In order to improve his sales technique, he realized that the prospect needed to do most of the talking. So he would ask himself, "Why am I talking?"

"You never won a game of tennis with the ball on your side of the court." ~ Steve Hall.

Ask questions twenty percent of the time and listen to answers eighty percent of the time. This strategy allows the prospect to decide for themselves whether to do business with you. When it's their idea, conversions increase dramatically, and buyer's remorse is almost non-existent. So when you're in a sales meeting, put away the PowerPoint presentation and start asking questions. Keep hitting the ball to them until you win.

"One good reason to always tell the truth. Honesty is much easier to keep track of." ~ John Maggio.

Life is just too busy and stressful to begin with. The thought of living two or three realities confuses the mind. One lie leads to another and another. You only have one reputation. Like my friend Pablo Alvarado Jr. of LPL Financial says; "You'll never have to tell a lie if you always tell the truth."

"The three rules to follow to be successful. 1. Is there a need for what you do? 2. Are you the best at it? 3. Can you be easily replaced?" ~ Andrew Shaffer of Andrew Shaffer Consulting".

Andrew's simple formula is the litmus test for all career moves. Is there even a market for what I want to do? Do you constantly improve and gain knowledge to be the best in your area of expertise? Logically and realistically, can you be easily replaced?

"Where your attention goes the energy flows" ~ Liz Clickner.

Retired school teacher, now a coach for retirees, Liz reminds us of this simple saying. If you keep thinking negative thoughts, negative things will happen in our lives. And, so is true of the opposite. Thoughts create feelings. Feelings create actions. Actions create results. Make sure you have positive feelings.

"Enjoy yourself; it's later than you think." ~ Jonathan (the day after his boss of 20 years passed)

Just a simple call to action to remind us to do what we love. Whether it's in our personal lives or professional, we can't waste time being unhappy, feeling negative, or being unproductive. We don't have that luxury.

Chapter 17
Keeping Your Momentum

Keep Making Mistakes

My son, who was nineteen at the time, posted something on social media. He must have been down on himself. He asked for forgiveness for making mistakes and not being perfect. I responded by saying that I was proud he had made so many mistakes. I explained the only real mistake would have been for him to sit on the couch and do nothing at all. I encouraged him to keep going and make mistakes as fast as he could make them.

In my mind, there are no mistakes if you are taking a risk outside of your comfort zone. Even after failure, we are victorious on so many levels. Every challenge, whether you win or lose, provides experience, wisdom, and knowledge.

Keep your perspective. A good batting average for a professional baseball player is thirty percent. In other words, they fail seventy percent of the time! In fact, the highest batting average in MLB History was in 1941 when Ted Williams finished the season with a .406 batting average. This statistic means he was missing almost sixty percent of the time. Today, top players are paid millions of dollars to "fail" most of the time. What language does the MLB use when discussing batting averages?

From the MLB Website. [Batting Average (AVG) Definition - One of the oldest and most universal tools to measure a hitter's success at the plate, the batting average is determined by dividing a player's hits by his total at-bats for a number between zero (shown as .000) and one (1.000).]

Notice that they do not use the word FAIL. They say, "at-bats."

It's all about the attempts. When coaching community basketball, we would tell the ten and eleven-year-old girls to take as many shots as they could. We would cheer madly every time they took a shot. Even though nine of ten shots missed, we all reacted with positive reinforcement. "Good shot, good shot!" All of the parents cheered each attempt. And, if a shot happened to go in, the auditorium erupted!

Instead of labeling yourself as failing or failure, try using different language. You took a shot. You attempted. You tried. There are no failures, only experiences. The biggest mistake you'll ever make is not to take a shot, make an attempt, or give it a try.

Thomas Edison, when inventing the light bulb, said: "I didn't fail, I just found 10,000 ways that didn't work."

Don't Wait

"...an imperfect plan implemented immediately and violently will always succeed better than a perfect plan" ~ General George S. Patton.

Take the opportunity, be imperfect, get out there, and make it happen. Often creating a perfect plan is one's way of hiding from committing to action. "We should wait; it's not perfect," or "Not yet, I have to do X first." Let's face it, more often than not, you are giving yourself an excuse to hide in your comfort zone.

We rationalize. We tell ourselves "rational lies" or worst yet, "a ration of lies." We are continually convincing ourselves to stay in our comfort zones out of sheer fear.

This book is a call to your accountability! Get your butt out there and start moving. Focus on your end goal and get going TODAY!

Brush Your Teeth

It amazes me what we choose to allow to go by the wayside. Often we start new routines hoping they will become habits. Maybe you wanted to start working out in the morning before work. Maybe you wanted to start to journal in the morning. Maybe you wanted to eliminate snacks after 7 pm. Many of these habits would greatly improve our lives, yet we often fall off the wagon and have a hard time getting back on track.

We still brush our teeth. If we wake up late, we don't skip; we brush our teeth. If you stay out late and forget to brush before bed, amazingly we start right back to brushing our teeth in the morning.

Why do we keep some rituals, yet give up on so many others that are beneficial to our future? Take time for yourself. Take time to journal. Make sure you exercise. Respect yourself enough to spend a few minutes on you first. If you want respect, you must show respect... to yourself.

Stay On Track

"Don't let the distractions become the attraction." ~ Casey Coven. Let's talk some more about distractions. The fastest way to a goal is a straight line. The reality is that real-world problems are bound to occur, causing you to adjust, restructure, and plot a new course of action. There is even a coined phrase for such occurrences, "Murphy's Law." These distractions are obvious.

1. Some obvious distractions. How many times have you spent too much time on your cell phone when you could have been working towards your dream? How many times have you binge-watched a Netflix series, but could have been taking steps towards your passion? How many relationships are distracting you from your goal? Distractions are the ultimate killer of dreams!

2. Negative Distractions. "You are the sum of the average of the five people you surround yourself with the most." Many of us encounter negativity in those we interact with personally and professionally. Some people are constantly trying to rob us of precious time to dwell on their behaviors and actions.

"Go where you're celebrated not where you're tolerated." - Unknown

3. Let's point out some not so obvious distractions. Back to eating your vegetables first! Or, as Brian Tracy said; Eat That Frog! Too often we are very productive, but not on the most direct track to our ultimate goal. "There is always work to do" as many mentors are prone to say. In your daily journey, you will encounter more distractions than you think.

Countless times I should have been writing this book, but instead, I was doing something else. Great stuff too! Creating great marketing for my company and going the extra mile for a client. Took meetings I didn't need to. Started cleaning around the office. The list is endless. All this while knowing all too well that writing this book would propel my career to the next level faster and more efficiently than all of those other activities combined.

Fear! Often, we skirt our responsibilities out of fear. Fear of achieving. Fear of not knowing what it looks like past that glass ceiling. Fear of leaving our comfort zones. As I write this very paragraph, I envision myself on stage speaking in front of the biggest room of my career. Not a hundred, but hundreds, or even thousands. Talk about scary! Even though it is where I want to go, the fear of failure is so great it has often kept me from finishing this very book.

Don't Sweat the Competition

Why would you want competitors around you? You should love the competition. Competition can help create the best you. Let me explain.

Ever been left out? Have you been picked last? The third wheel? Have you been bullied or been a bully to someone else? How did that feel? Why would we want to exclude anyone and make them feel the same?

People are like magnets. Sometimes there will be an instant attraction, and sometimes you will repel. We are all made up of energy with an electrical current running through our nervous systems.

In fact, competition is very healthy and good for not only our success but the success of the network around you. When faced with competition top performers will thrive tremendously.

Allow me to bring up a few examples. Look at your cell phone. What did your cell phone look like five years ago, ten years ago? When Apple went to market first with the iPhone, it started a smartphone war that we all benefited from in the end. Two major competitors, Apple and Android, started competing for market share. Six or more phone makers ended up duking it out to have the next big thing for the consumers.

One of the greatest promoters of all time, Vince McMahon of the WWF took advantage of competition every time it presented itself. He loved the surge in ratings that the competition created. Ultimately, Vince won each time and ended up consolidating his competition, WCW, and forming the WWE. I argue that he was able to win each time because he welcomed the competition and knew how to use the situation to his advantage. He envisioned the end before it even began.

Think of the advancements in industries surrounding you. Automotive, television, online shopping.... Competition has allowed these industries to thrive and benefit us all.

In the '90s and early 2000's many rejected the use of computers, saying they did not need to use them. They had lived all their lives just fine without computers. Within a decade, computers boomed, the internet happened, and now we all walk around with supercomputers in our pockets. Those who rejected computers were left behind in many ways. Competition and technology have completely changed the playing field for today's professional. Those who resist technology end up out of jobs. Companies that fail to evolve with technology go out of business.

There are NO DAYS OFF

You've got to work after work. Work before work. Work on your passion. Is it even "work" if you love what you're doing?

If you hate your 9-5, what are you doing from 5-9 to get out? Some are thinking 5 pm to 9 pm, but it can also be 5 am to 9 am. We've just identified eight hours that you can work on yourself so that you can get out of your self-described eight-hour hell hole. Don't be a slave to the grind… a rat in the race.

Your passion is like a hobby. You'll want to work on it all the time. You will think about it constantly. People stuck in a 9-to-5 mentality are not going to understand. The clock-punching mentality is too strong within their paradigms. Be ready for them to challenge you.

Some people say they want to sit on the beach for the rest of their lives. Some want to avoid having to work a grind. Not me, I just want to be free! What do you want?

A sure sign of your happiness is how you get out of bed in the morning. Do you wait until the last minute before getting out of bed? Do you sit on the edge of your bed and wish you didn't have to go to work? Do you mull around and deliberately take too long getting ready, making you habitually late? These are all signs you are not happy. It may be time to start looking for a new path.

Invest in Your Education and Success

The rule of thumb says that you should be investing three percent back into personal and professional development. When you learn this, you immediately think of money. While it takes some cash to learn and grow, consider that you also need to allow time for all of this to take place.

Some methods that you might explore to achieve this growth and forward movement include classes, workshops, networking events. Listen to podcasts and audiobooks, and do some reading. Business Expos are a great way to meet people in local markets.

Be consistent about making this investment in your development. It will pay huge dividends in your business efforts.

Say Yes To Opportunity

Saying yes to opportunity and maintaining a positive mindset is key. Things are easier than you think, once you move past your initial hesitation and get moving.

Life is like a box of... Legos! Did you play with Legos or puzzles as a child? Some children build houses, and now they are our architects. Some children build cars, and they are our auto mechanics. Some even built jets and spaceships who are now our pilots.

Everything is as simple as a few Legos! What if I told you that you could build or repair your own computer? If you brave enough to open the case, you will find that there are only a handful of components and they often only go together one way.

How about that oil change? Did you know it can be done in less than half a dozen steps? Most of the time we are simply too scared to look under the hood. Is the Lego analogy making sense now?

You can build anything with a box of Legos. You just have to get out there, roll up your sleeves, look under the hood, and do it.

The possibilities are endless if you don't limit your thinking. You can change the oil in your car. You can build furniture. You can master technology. You can construct a plan for moving your business forward.

Once you get past your initial hesitation and learn to say YES, YES gets easier and easier to say, and you will make a habit of being able to accomplish things. Conversely, if you get in the habit of doubting yourself and saying NO, you will be unable to move ahead the way you had planned and saying NO limits your ability to achieve.

Say Yes, Get in the Habit

Saying No to opportunities can become an easy habit to adopt, and hard to break. Don't succumb to this bad habit.

Momentum goes in both directions. The more you say No the easier it becomes to say it again. The more you decline an opportunity because you are afraid, the easier it will be to continue your losing streak. Each loss becomes easier than the last to accept. Eventually, you will feel like a loser.

Good News! That same momentum can help you succeed. When you say yes to opportunity it creates a feeling of empowerment. Each yes will lead to bigger and better opportunities. Even when difficult challenges present themselves, saying Yes will come with ease.

Most importantly, say YES to all opportunities that align with your ultimate goal - no matter what skill level they require, or what knowledge you may need to succeed. Things are much simpler than they seem. Just remember, everything is built from Legos.

Take Easy Wins, Measure At-Bats, not Home Runs. Take the next 365 days as 365 opportunities to say yes to success with local marketing.

About the Author

Michelle and John Maggio are the sister and brother team that own Hawk Marketing. They also serve as hosts of Networking in Annapolis. Networking in Annapolis is a series of local business events which provide everyone with the opportunity to connect, reconnect and network with local business professionals and entrepreneurs in the Annapolis MD area.

Helping local entrepreneurs, intrapreneurs, and network marketers win on a local level is a passion. Hosting 12-15 local networking events per month, John and Michelle present free workshops to local entrepreneurs.

Join the conversation on Facebook in the private group, "Networking in Annapolis".

Follow John Maggio at;
Facebook: https://www.facebook.com/johnmmaggio
Instagram: https://www.instagram.com/johnmaggio
LinkedIn: https://www.linkedin.com/in/johnmmaggio
Youtube: Search John Maggio

Follow Michelle Maggio at;
Facebook: https://www.facebook.com/michelle.mag...
Instagram: https://www.instagram.com/mcmaggio
LinkedIn: https://www.linkedin.com/in/michelle-...

For more information visit hawkmarketingservices.com.

Thank you all so very much, John & Michelle Maggio.

Made in the USA
Middletown, DE
31 October 2019